Anonymous

Jubilee of the London Society of Compositors

A brief record of events prior to and since its re-establishment in 1848

Anonymous

Jubilee of the London Society of Compositors
A brief record of events prior to and since its re-establishment in 1848

ISBN/EAN: 9783744730754

Printed in Europe, USA, Canada, Australia, Japan

Cover: Foto ©ninafisch / pixelio.de

More available books at **www.hansebooks.com**

JUBILEE OF THE LONDON SOCIETY OF COMPOSITORS

A BRIEF RECORD OF EVENTS

PRIOR TO AND SINCE ITS RE-ESTABLISHMENT IN 1848.

PRINTED FOR THE LONDON SOCIETY OF COMPOSITORS,
. BY .
BLADES, EAST & BLADES,
23, ABCHURCH LANE, E.C.

1898.

To the Members
of the
London Society of Compositors.

Gentlemen,

In preparing for the Members, on the occasion of the Society's Fiftieth Anniversary, a brief record of the work of the organisation to which they have the pleasure and privilege to belong, it has been found impossible to limit such review to the events which have occurred since its re-establishment in 1848. The solid and substantial work accomplished prior to that period not only laid the foundations of the existing Society as an organisation, but also produced the Scales of Prices which, although undergoing revision from time to time, have in certain essential particulars remained practically unaltered, besides crystallising customs which have since been generally recognised as binding both upon employers and employed. Therefore, to have confined the accompanying review to the proceedings of the past fifty years would have resulted in the presentation of an incomplete and indefinite record of events, thereby depriving the younger members of the opportunity of fully appreciating the will and determination with which their predecessors approached the task of endeavouring to improve the conditions under which their fellow-craftsmen were working.

Previous to the re-establishment of the Society, attempts had been made to form a united Trade Society, and although these efforts were attended with failure, the consequent disappointment but acted as an incentive to renewed and even more determined effort. It has to be remembered, also, that the difficulties and dangers which the earlier trade-unionists had to encounter were of a character which the present generation can hardly fully realise, but they will nevertheless recognise the sturdy services rendered to the cause of Unionism by those whose efforts eventually succeeded in establishing the present Society.

In reviewing the history of our organisation, if there is one feature which stands out in bolder relief than another, it is the desire which, on all occasions and under all circumstances, has been evinced by the members in favour of a signed and sealed working agreement with their employers. This feeling cannot be said to have been stronger at one period than at another—on the contrary, it has been the most consistent and striking feature of the Society's policy, and may be said to have proved to be the keystone of its influence and of its steady and continuous prosperity.

The records also clearly prove that the members have never been content to adopt a "rest and be satisfied" policy, ample evidence being forthcoming of their sustained efforts to improve the organisation, by the addition of new or the increasing of old benefits—happily, seldom in the direction of reducing them.

It is not to be supposed that this or any other society could take upon itself heavy liabilities in the shape of numerous benefits, without at times being called upon to consider the question of "ways and means;" but whenever the necessity has arisen for consulting members upon the financial position, they have at all times responded to the call made upon them in the most ready and generous manner. Notably has this been the case when dealing with the claims of their unemployed brethren, and it may safely be asserted that the records of the Society in this direction cannot be surpassed by those of any other organisation with a similar membership.

There are other features of the Society's work—such as the financial assistance rendered to various trades in times of stress, the amounts annually granted in aid of medical and trade charities, and particularly the comparatively small expenditure in strike benefit during the past fifty years—which might, perhaps, be dwelt upon with advantage, but as these and other items have been fully set forth in the accompanying pages, members will be able to form their own conclusions upon matters the contemplation of which cannot give rise to other than the most agreeable impressions.

Upon an occasion like the present, it is but natural that members should congratulate each other upon the excellent position to which the Society has attained, after fifty years of useful and progressive work; but in so doing it may be taken for granted that they will not forget the efforts of those members who in earlier days upheld the standard of Unionism at a time when liberty of speech—much less of person—was not so secure as now, but whose determination materially assisted to build up the association of which the members, as a body, have such reason to be proud.

To the younger men, the records of the Society's history cannot prove to be other than interesting and instructive, and will doubtless stimulate them to renewed activity in their endeavours to maintain and, if possible, excel the good work of those who have preceded them; whilst the "pioneers" of the Society will have the satisfaction of knowing that their early struggles and successes are not unappreciated by those on whose behalf

I have the honour to remain,

Faithfully yours,

C. W. BOWERMAN,
Secretary.

7-9, St. Bride Street,
   Ludgate Circus, E.C.,
      July 9th, 1898.

EVENTS PRIOR TO THE RE-ESTABLISHMENT OF THE SOCIETY.

ONE of the earliest of the Society's records of the London printing trade is the Report of a Committee appointed by the News Society of Compositors "to draw up a statement of the regular Mode of Working on Newspapers, for the Information of the Trade; to examine documents, and to report the same." The Report was presented on the 29th of July, 1820, and bears the signatures of Messrs. P. Chalk, H. Warren, E. M. Davis, W. Yockney, T. Paterson, and J. P. Spence. The instructions to the Committee directed them to "give a fair scale of work, mode, time, and price, on all newspapers, wherever published," and involved an examination of "the bases of all official agreements, and all acknowledged and understood rules;" and in their Report the Committee claimed that they had particularly adhered to their instructions by keeping in view "that it was to guide the ignorant, to prevent the evil intentions of the unprincipled, and, if possible, to form a closer bond of union among yourselves." Considerable time must have been devoted to the task, the Committee commencing their labours by tracing the

Regulations for News Work prevailing during the preceding fifty years, "in order to support them in their declaration that they had been introduced on fair principles, that they had been cordially agreed to by the Masters, had been acted upon by the employed for so great a length of time, and that any innovation made on those regulations by an employer, or set of men acting for themselves without the concurrence of the general body of news compositors, should be opposed, and those concerned in such an attempt treated as enemies to their fellow workmen, and marked as acting inimically to the interests of their profession." The Report traces the gradual growth of newspaper work from 1770, the various changes which had been made in the methods of production, and the variations made from time to time in the rates of wages and hours of working, both of news-men and book-hands.

It records that on the 14th January, 1793, a Circular was issued by the latter, claiming payment for "head and direction lines of pages, and the en and em quadrats at the sides," the employers agreeing to the first proposal, thus relieving the bookwork compositors of an "intolerable grievance." With regard to newspaper work, minion type had been introduced, the old method of display had been discarded, a new taste had appeared in the arrangement of the matter in the inner form, and the former advertisement style "was completely exploded." The Report further states that from 1785 to 1793, owing to the strong competition for public favour, newspapers underwent a most material alteration. "It was a remarkable epoch, including the most eventful seven years of the last century. The disarrangements, both civil and political, concomitant to a return to peace after a long war, had caused a strong political feeling in the public mind ; of course, information from all quarters was eagerly sought, and as readily given by the editors of the daily journals, among whom, as with their readers, party spirit rose to its utmost height, and no expense was spared to gratify it. In this period, nineteen new journals put forth their claims for public support—the majority, however, were 'born but to die !' Two of the older papers also expired ; but their places were occupied by seven juniors." One journal "went beyond the rest," by introducing French rules, small capitals for particular paragraphs, and discarding nearly all the double letters, and the long *s*.

On the 19th of May, 1809, a Circular was addressed "To the Proprietors of Newspapers," requesting an advance of one-fifth- -8*s*. per week on morning, and 6*s*. per week on evening papers—and pointing out that when, in 1801, an advance of one-sixth was obtained on all works in book houses, those employed upon newspapers did not receive a proportionate rise. The Circular (which was accompanied by the first and regular "Scale for News Work," and was signed by 198 newsmen) stated "that this circumstance, together with the great increase of labour on papers of late years, arising from the introduction of so large a portion of small letter, are considerations which, we hope, will not be passed over without that deliberation they deserve. From an impartial view of the comparative statements and the proposed advance, it will be seen that we have kept perfectly within the limits prescribed by justice. We have pursued this line of conduct from a solicitude to avoid the introduction of anything which might prevent your ready compliance with our request." The terms asked for were £2 8s. for morning, and £2 3s. for evening paper hands (ten hours' composition to be the specific time for the latter). No reply being forthcoming from the employers, a second Circular was sent to them, on the 13th of June, signed by the same number of men; this likewise being ignored, on the 20th of June the men handed in their notices, but before the fortnight had expired "each journeyman received a copy of a Report of a Committee of Masters, dated June 30th, accompanied by a string of resolutions, but not meeting the request of the men."

The employers' meeting took place at the "Turk's Head" Coffee House, Strand, representatives attending from five morning and five evening papers, "to consider the report of the Committee appointed to inquire into and report their opinion upon the Circular Letter of the Compositors respecting certain alleged grievances, and demanding an advance of wages." The employers' reply was embodied in eleven paragraphs, and was accompanied by a comparative Table of the Prices of Necessaries, from 1793 to 1809, in contradiction to that compiled by the journeymen. The first paragraph condemned the strong spirit evinced by the men in demanding so large a rise as 20 per cent., and protested against the proposed scale as containing "rules and restrictions new to the trade, and embarrassing to the proprietors, while no reciprocal benefit or advantage is held out." The second attempted to controvert the assertion of the newsmen that they "experienced difficulties in procuring the necessaries of life," by declaring it "a matter of surprise and regret that anything so unfounded should be advanced on so serious an occasion by a body of men, generally speaking, so intelligent and respectable;" and after comparing their wages with those paid to book-hands, stated "that their claims to high wages do not rest on the difficulties in obtaining the necessaries of life, but on the disagreeable hours of labour. They make more money than falls to the lot of 39-40ths of the men in Britain, and they can procure not only all the necessaries of life, but even more of its comforts than ninety-nine out of every hundred men in Europe. It is lamentable to see men so insensible to the blessings of their situation."

The sixth paragraph states that "the reference made to the increased labour on newspapers, in consequence of the introduction of small letter, is unjust, is absurd, and we cannot understand how they could allow so unfounded a complaint to escape them. The proprietors have always paid, and paid smartly too, for this introduction. The compositors have limited hours of employment, limited quantities of work, and they compose only one number of letters, whether small or large, agreeably to the universal rule of the business." The eighth recommended that "the false assertions, groundless complaints, and extravagant pretensions of the compositors should be met by a firm and determined resistance," and for fear that they (the compositors) should be intoxicated by success to demand "double wages," stated "that they have therefore considered a plan of establishing a Society of Compositors under an Act of Parliament, connecting with it a benefit society, which, they are confident, will enable the trade to go on, and which they may hereafter submit to you." Finally, after expressing indignation at what they considered to be the extravagant demands of the men, the employers recommended that they should receive a rise proportionate to that obtained by the book-hands in 1801—2s. to morning and 1s. to evening paper hands, but without reducing the hours of composition demanded from the latter.

During the following year the book-hands secured an advance of one-seventh in their prices, which took effect on the 1st of May. The newsmen then asked for a similar rise, but, as the request remained unnoticed, they determined to press the matter, the book-hands supporting them by passing a resolution that, pending a settlement of the dispute, no one should be permitted to apply for employment upon a newspaper. The employers then offered a rise of 4s. to morning and 3s. to evening paper hands. These terms were refused, and the customary notices tendered by the men, but on the last day of the fortnight they were informed by their respective Printers that the demands had been agreed to, and that in future the scale for morning papers would be £2 8s. (galley 3s. 10d. per thousand), and for evening papers £2 3s. 6d. (galley 3s. 7d. per thousand). It will thus be seen that the Scale-price per thousand for which the compositors of 1810 so persistently and energetically fought, has remained the standard rate down to the present moment.

In those days—as in more modern times—men who took a prominent part in conducting the negotiations on behalf of their fellow members occasionally incurred the resentment of their employers, and were, on some pretext or other, dismissed from their situations. Arising out of this dispute, however, the consequences to some of the men concerned therein were much more serious. Although eleven of the newspaper proprietors had granted the memorial (which had been presented to them and supported by the men in the manner sanctioned by the custom of the trade), the other—the proprietor of the most influential journal of that, as it is of the present, period—refused to be bound by the terms of the agreement which had been accepted by his fellow-employers; this refusal being followed by the prosecution of eleven of the members, who were indicted on a charge of conspiracy, and sentenced to twelve months' imprisonment in Newgate Gaol. Unhappily, one of the members (Malcolm Craig) fell a victim to his punishment; whilst another (J. Simpson) was, happily, spared to assist in starting the "London Union of Compositors" in 1834, thus giving practical proof that his incarceration in prison in 1810 had not weakened his ardour in the cause of trade unionism. Although in point of time the incident may appear to belong to a remote period, when such prosecutions were by no means unusual, it must, after all, be remembered that it is only in comparatively recent years that the law of combination has been sufficiently broadened to prevent such vindictive actions being brought against workmen by their employers; and it should therefore not be difficult to realise the storm of indignation which was felt by our predecessors at the treatment meted out to their comrades, as evidenced by the stirring words used by the Committee of the day in reporting upon the matter. " Torn from their families, separated from their associates, months rolled over them in the gloom of a prison. Their brethren were alive to their sufferings; they felt, they commiserated; and what comfort they could afford was cheerfully given, and as gratefully received. This unfortunate circumstance is still in your memories; cherish it; and when sinking in the vale of years, may the sufferers be enlivened by the smiles of their younger brethren, and ever be remembered when parted from us! . . . The glow of sympathy shall rouse us to despise their persecutor, and encourage us in maintaining the cause for which they suffered."

After chronicling the fact that about the year 1813 morning papers of twenty columns became almost general, and that the increase in size "had not rendered the use of small type less necessary than when they consisted of but sixteen columns," the Report proceeds to state that at the commencement of the year 1816 "the trade was thrown into confusion by the introduction of nonpareil, a type not recognised in former agreements respecting the price for newspaper work. The companionship were required to compose it at minion price and quantity they refused, and in consequence left their situations; but others, in direct opposition to the interests of the profession, submitted to the demand. Ignorance could not be pleaded by them, for your Committee are well aware that few men can be found incapable of casting up the galley on a newspaper, or be unacquainted with the difference in price of nonpareil and other types used in book-houses. The bad example set by these men, with the desire of gain, may have induced others to follow their steps; but they cannot, unless you lose your unanimity, sap the foundations of your rights. It is therefore incumbent upon your Committee to protest against any men taking upon themselves the right of deviating from your regulations, or of settling either the price or quantity of the galley of smaller type than minion, without a general understanding with their brethren of the profession. It has caused both trouble and expense, and been the means of removing good men to gratify the meanness or greediness of those who have in the end been necessitated to throw themselves upon the mercy of their fellow-workmen, for permission to gain a subsistence among those they had, by their previous conduct, deprived of bread." The negotiations resulted in the recognition of the proportionate value prevailing in book-houses—1*d*. per thousand extra.

Towards the close of the same year a misunderstanding arose in consequence of a morning and evening paper being produced in the same office. On the 3rd of January, 1817, the dispute was considered at a delegated meeting of news compositors, held at the "Coach and Horses," Water Lane, Fleet Street, when it was resolved "that there are but three classes of workmen on morning papers that can be acknowledged by the profession—full hands, £2 8*s*. per week; supernumeraries, £1 3*s*. per week; and assistants, at 11½*d*. per hour; that we consider the situation of finishers on a morning paper (where no person is employed to do the preceding part of the work) as an innovation that would tend to disorganise the system hitherto acted upon; that under this consideration we recommend to our fellow-workmen to refuse any such situation should it be offered them; and that with respect to the journal under consideration (having no precedent to act upon, and there not being a regular companionship), we recommend to the persons employed thereon to regulate the trifling difference between them and their employer as amicably as possible, keeping in view that the interests of the profession are not invaded thereby."

The term "finishers" will be better understood when it is stated that in the following year a dispute arose on another journal, by a demand being made for eleven hours' work (time and quantity)—or two measured galleys and a finish, sometimes extending to three hours. This mode of working was declared inadmissible by the trade, and successfully resisted "by the sacrifice of situation only of those that refused their acquiescence."

No other question of general interest appears to have arisen until May, 1820, when the Committee were called upon to consider the result of the dispute which occurred four years previously. They report as follows: "After the introduction of nonpareil on the journal mentioned in the year 1816, the trade were ignorant of the men and their modes of work; you had no interest in the inquiry, for they never could be respected who had deserted your standard, nor pitied when labouring under difficulties they had brought upon themselves. From an accidental occurrence, not necessary here to repeat, a request was made that a statement of the situation of that journal might be laid before you. Policy dictated the propriety of receiving it—if those employed acted up to the spirit of your laws, you would have nothing to condemn; but if, on the contrary, they had violated your system, you would have the opportunity of declaring against it, and of preventing the evil example from spreading further. Custom, it is said, will in time become law; so would your silence have permitted the unprincipled to gratify themselves by the sacrifice of your rights and interests, and to undermine your whole system before you were aware of the danger."

From the statement presented by the non-society men—who presumably were dissatisfied with the conditions under which they were working—it was ascertained that two modes of employment prevailed in this particular office, both in direct opposition to the rules and prices agreed upon in 1810. On account of the quantity of advertisements, two companionships had been formed, one for the outer and another for the inner form—*i.e.*, a 'ship to produce the news matter, and necessarily employed at night; the advertisements being set in the daytime, by a distinct 'ship. The latter had accepted an evening paper price per galley for nonpareil, minion quantity; the night hands being employed in agreement with the custom and terms recognised by the trade. "It is unnecessary," the Committee state, "to comment upon the introduction of two companionships on a daily paper, much less to point out the absurdity of consenting to receive an evening paper price on a morning journal, upon the plea of its being performed by daylight; by the same parity of reasoning, the morning paper price might be demanded for an evening journal because, for a great part of the year, a portion of the work is done by candlelight." The steps (if any) taken by the non-society men to induce the employer to fully recognise the scale and custom of the trade are not stated; but shortly afterwards an alteration in the inner form system was proposed —viz., two galleys and remaining until the paper went to press—which was refused by the men, with the result that "seven out of twelve deserted this 'flag of blackest hue.'"

In view of the consequences that might probably follow the circumstances just recorded, a committee (from whose exhaustive report the preceding facts have been gathered) was appointed to draw up and circulate, for the information of the trade, a statement of the regular mode of working on newspapers—"to guide the ignorant, to guard the unwary." To assist this committee, "and to maintain that harmony which should ever subsist between two branches in one profession," a request was submitted to a delegated meeting of bookmen for "the appointment of a gentleman from their body to assist them in the task assigned, which was most cheerfully met and cordially assented to."

Shortly after their appointment, their labours were added to through "the proprietor of an obscure evening journal, out of which a Sunday paper is formed, making a demand on the employed to complete the weekly journal, not merely with a reduction of wages, but absolutely for nothing!— as a kind of make-weight for the salary they received upon the other." This the companionship refused to do, with the result that they were discharged, "their places being filled by some *distinguished* characters, now out of the pale, but whose memories will be cherished."

After enumerating the variations which had taken place in the methods of working, together with the advantages gained by the workmen, during the fifty years embraced in their report, "in which is included fifteen years prior to the date of the first document," reference is made to the effort of the newsmen in 1793 to obtain an advance of wages, "which, though sanctioned by the signatures of their brethren in the Book Department, your Committee consider as the first division of the compositors into two branches of one profession." Although an equal advance was sought for all daily paper hands, the rise gained for morning paper work was 1 7th (or 4s. 6d.), and for evening paper work 1 13th (or 2s. 6d.), "and your Committee cannot pass over the distinction then made between morning and evening papers without expressing their regret at the circumstance." The resolutions against the employment of apprentices on newspapers were passed the same year, the practice having been to employ them on many journals, especially weekly papers, both classes of work being produced in book-houses; but when in 1793 "daily papers required separate establishments, and were conducted by non-professional men, your brethren took the opportunity of objecting to their re-admission on the latter class." Owing to the altered conditions of working, and consequent increase of labour in evening paper offices, during the preceding seven years, in 1800 a resolution was passed and (with one exception) generally accepted, "That all composition cease when the day's publication goes to press—all work afterwards to be paid for as extra, or deducted from the first work of the next day's publication." A regulation was also passed governing the quantity of work to be produced by morning paper hands in the twelve hours. After drawing up an "Abstract of the Scale, with the Laws and necessary Regulations attached," the Committee conclude by stating : "You require nothing of the employers—they demand nothing from you; and shall it be said that your privileges must be forfeited by your own negligence, be scattered into air by the unprincipled, or sacrificed to the interest of a designing few ? Forbid it, spirit ! while the recollection of the struggles of our predecessors lives amongst us!" It is worthy of note that the subscribers' (or members') names attached to this official statement (July, 1820) numbered but 193.

It is evident, therefore, that although the first Trade Society (which was formed in 1810) comprised but about one-third of the compositors then employed in London, the members were animated by the truest and strongest spirit of unionism, and faced the various struggles with every desire to consider the reasonable objections that might be raised by the employers, but determined at the same time to leave no stone unturned in order that the status of their fellow-workmen might be improved. The Scales formulated by them (both for book and newsmen) not only proved to be the foundation of all succeeding Scales, but became for a series of years the only acknowledged regulations governing the trade, and although, in the natural course of time and events, the rates improved from time to time, the general principles upon which they were based remain to this day practically unchanged.

Prior to the formation of the Trade Society, compositors had no other remedy for their wants and grievances than by forwarding to their employers signed documents the result being that in course of time each office had its own particular method of charging, rendering it difficult, if not impossible, to determine which of the various practices was right, and consequently advantageous to the interests of the trade as a whole. But within four years of the starting of the Society in 1805—the members succeeded in obtaining the co-operation of the employers in the formation of an Arbitration Committee, eight representatives being appointed by each side "to frame regulations for the future payment of the compositors' work." From the labours of this Committee a Scale resulted—comprising twenty-seven articles—which, after being slightly altered in 1810, formed the basis of charges until the year 1847.

After being mainly instrumental in producing so valuable and comprehensive a Scale, the Trade Society appears to have crumbled to pieces, with the result that six years later the employers were successful in enforcing a reduction of $\frac{3}{4}d$. per thousand upon reprints. The Report upon the Scale presented in 1847 states that "this reduction is remarkable for two things 1. That sixteen years prior, the employers absolutely refused to accede to a proposition put before them by the men, asking for an increase upon manuscript, and at the same time a distinction to be made between manuscript and reprint in the price per thousand; 2. That the document which enforced this alteration of what was called in 1800 'an unjustifiable departure from the established and long-approved principles by which works have been appreciated,' was signed by twenty masters only, the men not being consulted, nor their remonstrances heeded when they sought for a definition of the ambiguous term 'reprint.'" This action of the employers was followed by a strike, which, however, proved abortive to resist the threatened reduction; and from that period until 1847 the Scale remained unaltered.

On the 1st of May, 1826, was formed The London General Trade Society of Compositors. With other and probably to some extent rival societies dividing the trade, it was naturally but a question of time when circumstances would arise rendering united action not only desirable, but absolutely necessary. Expression appears to have been given to this feeling in an Address issued by the Committee on May 1st, 1833, which will be read with interest, despite the fact that sixty-five years have elapsed since the appeal was addressed to the Compositors of London:

"ADDRESS.

"In the year 1826, several active and intelligent individuals, convinced of the inefficiency of the then existing institution to protect the rights of the trade, and anxious to secure the wages of the journeyman from any such unjust reduction as had been made upon reprints, deliberated on the practicability of forming a society which, by being suited to the views and conditions of all, might be worthy of *general* support, and combine at once the energies and the talents of the trade. After having maturely considered the subject, they called a general meeting of the trade, to which they submitted the plan they had prepared for the establishment of a society, to be called The London General Trade Society, which, after discussion, received the sanction of the meeting, consisting of about fifteen hundred persons. A few interested and influential, but short-sighted, individuals were, however, opposed to the measure thus generally sanctioned, and the infant society had to struggle with difficulties which could not perhaps have been overcome, had it not been founded upon the purest principles of liberality and justice; but the structure being thus based, as it were, upon a rock, withstood the united assaults of falsehood, fraud, and violence; and from that day until the present it has been continually making advances, converting enemies into friends, and accumulating resources, until at length, having put to silence, by its liberality and rectitude, the tongues of the malicious and malignant, it now stands forth as a Trade Society pre-eminent for its excellence and usefulness.

"To those who are ignorant of the proceedings of the London General Trade Society from its establishment in 1826 to the present period (1833), it is considered advisable to state that, since its commencement, not one member has quitted it on account of its mismanagement, its tardiness, inefficiency, or illiberality—its numbers have always been increasing—its receipts have been augmenting every year, and never has it been found necessary to withdraw its money from the public funds, although it has always paid its full proportion of all trade expenses, and has invariably been the foremost to reward those who have been injured in their attempts to maintain the rights of the trade.

"The proceedings of the Society are openly conducted - no secret and partial investigations—no party decisions have ever stained its records—no wasteful expenditure or embezzlement of its receipts can ever take place- its accounts are publicly audited every quarter—its acts, its funds, its laws, are under the control of its members, who can at all times investigate or take part in the direction of its affairs. Its constitution is at once so simple and vigorous, yet so admirably framed to meet every circumstance that may arise, that it is enabled to afford the best advice in all cases of dispute with employers; it gives the most prompt assistance to all who need it—no tedious delays, no useless formalities fetter its proceedings, but it grants to its members immediate pecuniary aid and legal assistance, whenever such support and advice are required.

"Since, then, it must be admitted by all, that those who live by their labour ought to unite to secure to themselves the just wages of labour, and since experience has shown that the disposition of masters in general is to grant the lowest possible remuneration for labour; and knowing, also, that without union amongst men, it is always in the power of employers to deprive their workmen of even a proper share of the common necessaries of life—it is a duty which every man owes to himself and to his family, to take such steps as shall secure to him the proper reward of his industry. This just reward, however, cannot be obtained by individual exertion—it is union alone that can effect it. The only security to the workman from injustice, oppression, and pauperism, is a well-conducted Trade Society; and as seven years' experience has proved that for promptitude of action, liberality of character, and stability of government, the London General Trade Society stands proudly pre-eminent, the Compositors of London are earnestly invited to come forward and give to that society the support to which it is strictly entitled, and which it has always received from those who have investigated its merits.

"The present, as well as the prospective, interests of the trade require union. No effective and permanent remedy can be found for the existing inequality of prices, the chicaneries of petty masters, the numerous wilful misinterpretations of the Scale, the evils of the present out-door apprentice system, turnovers, etc., until all the Compositors of London have become members of a Trade Society; and as the London General Trade Society is peculiarly calculated to be the instrument which shall remove these long-endured grievances, it becomes the imperative duty of all to strengthen the number of that society, and thus hasten the period of their removal; and in urging the Compositors of London to take this step, it is only considered necessary, in conclusion, to remark that the efficiency of the London General Trade Society is not weakened by a variety of objects and a diversity of interests—it is truly a Trade Society, since it has but one object in view—namely, the protection of the wages of labour; and those who desire to reap the just reward of their industry, to correct the evils arising from the illiberality and avarice of selfish employers, and secure for themselves a never-failing shelter from powerful and wealthy disputants, should, without further delay, enrol their names on the list of its members."

Members were admitted by ballot, after being duly proposed and seconded, on the first Monday in the month, the Committee and the members present exercising the

power of admission or rejection. The entrance fee was
1s. 6d., with a subscription of one penny per week, and
4d. per quarter towards defraying expenses of management. Strike payments ranged from 2s. (after two
years' membership) to 5s. (after five years' membership)
per week. The Society's business was conducted by a
Committee of eight, who met every Monday night, from
8.30 to 10.30, receiving 2s. for refreshments; and on
monthly, quarterly and special meeting nights, 3s.

The rules of this Society (as amended and unanimously
sanctioned on the 31st of May, 1832) also provided for
the payment of "its moiety of necessary expenses" in
furtherance of the objects of the Union Committee,
whose assistance it could claim "in all cases of difficulty
or peculiarity." Any member or Chapel feeling dissatisfied with the decision of their own Committee, had
the right to refer the matter in dispute to the Union
Committee, "whose decision is to be considered the
Act of this Society, and binding on the parties."

This Committee (which was termed "The Union
Committee of the London Trade Societies of Compositors") had been appointed in agreement with
resolutions passed at a General Meeting of the London
Trade Societies of Compositors, and consisted of twelve
members (six from each society), to whom all important
trade questions were to be referred, their decision to be
binding upon newspaper as well as book offices. They
were empowered to call in the advice of the officers of
the respective societies, or of such other persons as they
deemed necessary, the expense of their fortnightly meetings, etc., being defrayed out of the funds of each society.

They were prevented by rule from assuming any legislative authority, "being a Committee of final appeal and consultation, and not an executive body." The Union Committee were not permitted "to print or to deliver summonses, or to make profit in any way whatever, directly or indirectly, of any order or business they may find necessary to have done, thereby keeping themselves above suspicion and setting an example by the rectitude of their motives and transactions."

The importance of the task entrusted to the Union Committee will be gathered from the following instruction embodied in the resolutions passed at the meeting which brought the Committee into existence: "That as soon after their assembling as convenient, the Union Committee shall take into its most serious consideration the Compositors' Scale, in order that some plan may be adopted for more clearly elucidating those parts of it which, on account of their present ambiguity, often create misunderstanding between journeymen and their employers." In order that this important work might be done, they were further empowered by resolution "to provide a book for the alphabetical entry of the various customs and regulations of the trade, that they may no longer be deemed as matters of opinion; but will thus, by degrees, become settled laws of the composing branch of the business, the ignorance of which not only cause men to disagree with each other, but too frequently give opportunities to many selfish employers or other interested persons to introduce into printing offices customs and regulations at variance with the more established rules of the business. This book, appended to an elucidation of the Scale, would, in two or three years, become the text-book of the trade, and would often be as gladly referred to as an authority by the masters as by the men."

In the Report of the Journeymen Members of the Conference of Master Printers and Compositors, held in 1847, reference is made to the results of the Union Committee's labours, as follows : " In 1834, under the auspices of the late London Union, a commentary was appended to the Scale, which for information and clear reading could not be too highly prized. Subsequently an appendix was added, exceedingly useful to the compositor. But the 'Green Book,' as this Scale is commonly termed, had one defect—it was the compositors', not the masters' and compositors' book. Master printers would not acknowledge it because journeymen made it ; and thus, while it has been a valuable guide to the compositor, it has been of no service to him as an accepted authority by his employer. Numberless disputes have originated upon the wording of the Scale itself ; but those which have produced the most serious consequences concerned not so much charges that were in the Scale as those that were left out of it."

One of the most important of these "omissions" had reference to the question of periodical publications (other than monthlies or quarterlies), and the difficulty of defining whether such work should be done under the newspaper scale, or under the scale governing book work. This important matter occupied the attention of a special delegate meeting of the trade, held at the

"Red Lion," Red Lion Court, Fleet Street, on October 9th, 1832, when the Union Committee presented a report embodying six propositions, having as their object "to devise the best mode of checking the existing evils, and securing the rights of the compositor from infringement." At this meeting there were present 138 delegates from book houses, and representatives from two newspaper offices (the "Herald" and "True Sun"). The report stated that about fifty of these periodicals were being produced weekly, or at shorter periods, employing about 200 hands, the success attending "The Poor Man's Guardian" and "The Penny Magazine" having produced many rivals and imitators. Prior to the matter being referred to the Union Committee, the dissatisfaction and differences of opinion felt by the compositors had caused one of the societies to appoint a Committee of Inquiry, who found "that such a general departure from the usages of the trade had taken place upon several of the penny publications, and even annuals, as is truly alarming to us as a society, and to the profession at large."

By the time the Union Committee's report had been read, the room had become so overcrowded that an adjournment took place until the 16th of October, when the delegates assembled at the "Hope" Tavern, Blackmoor Street, Clare Market, when the report was again read, and after three of the propositions had been discussed, another adjournment took place until the 23rd October, at the same place, when an agreement was arrived at upon four of the six propositions, the resolutions defining that (1) publications or parts thereof, when pulled in galley, should be made up at the expense of the employer ; (2) publications containing two bodies (not being notes) to be cast up to the respective founts and charged the 2s. 6d. allowed by Article VII. of the Scale; (3) all publications which appear weekly, or at shorter periods, whether stamped or unstamped, which contain general news, such as parliamentary reports, reports of police or law courts, foreign or provincial intelligence, reports of daily occurrences, or notices of bankrupts, to be paid according to the existing Scale for Newspapers; but all those which contain only reviews of books, notices of dramatic or musical performances, articles on the fine arts, accounts of the meetings and proceedings of religious, literary, or scientific societies, and advertisements, to be paid the same as monthly or quarterly publications ; (4) that no companionship allow its work to be made up by an individual on the establishment, or in any other way effect a compromise with the employer, contrary to the usage of the trade."

An important Delegate Meeting was held at the same house on the 12th December, 1833, when 185 representatives were present from book houses employing 1,200 journeymen, and delegates from seven daily paper offices. At this meeting a letter was read from the "Courier" office, stating that "the companionship informed the Secretaries of the Trade Societies that they must decline to send delegates to the meeting of this evening, in consequence of the vagueness of the notice which they have received, and the irregular manner in which it reached them ; conceiving, as they do, that the notice should have been communicated to the Secretary of the News Committee, and through him to the different chapels. The 'Courier' companionship beg, however, to state that, should the object of the meeting be one which will tend to the general benefit of the business, they will be very ready to co-operate in its accomplishment. The 'Courier' companionship deem it necessary to make this communication, to prevent any supposition of intentional negligence."

The report of the Union Committee, after remarking that since the trade was called together in October, 1832, "they have had several causes for convening an Assembly of Delegates, but, fearful that the continued meetings of the trade would excite attention, and be the means of calling into action persons whose interests are in some respects opposed to those of the compositors of London," goes on to say that "they have deferred the meeting until the present period, when honesty, justice, and the preservation of a good understanding amongst compositors demand that it should be deferred no longer." After submitting their first financial statement, which stated that they had received £6 4s. 4d. from the Trade Society, and £9 3s 11d. from the General Trade Society, explanations were given respecting certain disputes which had arisen notably, the claim of the companionship of the "Penny Magazine" to the whole of the cuts appearing in the completed volume — and the inability of the Union Committee to adequately support or compensate members of the Trade Societies who had sacrificed or lost their situations through carrying out the decisions of the Union Committee.

The engagement of casual hands at 6d. per hour (which it was declared was contrary to the custom of the business), and the charge to be made for work set up in more than one measure, were also reviewed; also the question whether compositors receiving stated weekly wages "are bound to light up candles before the usual time, without receiving extra pay." Another subject into which the Committee had inquired was "How the present rate of establishment wages became fixed at 33s.," and it was ascertained "that previously to the reduction of the reprints in 1816, the lowest recognised price for establishment men was 36s. (for ten hours per day); but at that period a reduction of 3s. per week was also effected in the establishment wages, which reduction was considered to be somewhere about the loss that would be sustained by individuals working on the piece upon reprints."

The portion of the report, however, which the Committee considered to be of "infinitely greater importance" than the subjects already mentioned, and one upon which "the just regulation and prosperity of the business must in future mainly depend," contained an invitation to the delegates "to the consideration of some plan for establishing a Union of the Compositors of London, by which the better defence of their interests, and the general improvement of the business may be secured." For nearly twenty years, it was stated, Trade Societies had been established, and "yet not more than one-third of the trade had ever contributed to their support;" and it was under these circumstances, and after duly recognising the good work done by the existing societies, that the Union Committee had taken upon themselves the responsibility of submitting the proposition "That a portion of the delegates of the present meeting be appointed to confer with the Union Committee and the officers of the Trade Societies, in order that a plan may be arranged for uniting the existing societies, and enrolling the whole trade, in one society, under one head." The proposal (as also one imposing a levy of 1s. 6d.) met with the heartiest approval of the delegates, there being but one dissentient, and twelve members were appointed by the meeting to act with the Union Committee and the trade officials.

On the 4th and 11th of March, 1834, meetings were held in the theatre of the Mechanics' Institution, to receive a "Report from the General Trade Committee to the Compositors of London." Letters were read from both societies expressing the approval of their members (by resolutions passed at specially convened meetings) at the proposed plan of union, and pledging themselves, individually and collectively, to use their utmost exertions and influence to promote the object in view. A double delegated meeting of the daily paper men had also been held, who resolved "that if the members of the Union will so far modify their rules as to allow a full jurisdiction to the News Society in matters affecting their own body alone, and not interfering with the trade at large, they (the News Society) will, at the earliest opportunity, consider their proposal with every view to meet the interests of the trade at large." In agreement with this suggestion, the Committee proposed "that on the last Saturday in each month the Trade Council shall assemble for the purpose of considering all questions affecting newspapers; on which occasions a delegate shall attend from each of the daily newspaper offices, and form a part of the Council for that evening; and that for the purpose of aiding in the registration of the decisions on these evenings, a person employed on one of the daily papers shall be appointed to the office of assistant registrar." This suggestion, however, was not favourably considered, which led the Union Committee to declare that the newsmen had no right to a separate jurisdiction, on the ground that they held their situations "by the tenure of a fortnight's warning," and that as "bookmen may become newsmen in a few days," the latter had no right to legislate for the former, "where wages would depend upon their decision, without the bookmen having a voice in such decision."

The Committee further contended that the wages of newsmen did not depend upon a union amongst themselves, but upon the aid and co-operation of the bookmen; urging that they never obtained a rise until after the bookmen had gained it; that when apprentices were ejected from daily paper offices "the resolutions on the subject were sent round the book trade for the sanction, concurrence, or disapproval of the bookmen, without whose assistance they could not have ejected them;" and that without the aid of the bookmen "they never would or could have obtained the final adjustment of their prices, for, in order to carry this, it was necessary for the members of the book trade to come to a resolution that no bookman should apply for a situation on a newspaper during the dispute," thus proving that the object was gained, not by the union of the newsmen alone, but by the union of the news and bookmen.

c

The outcome of these meetings was the adoption of eighteen Articles on the Rules and Regulations for a General Union of the Compositors, to be called "The London Union of Compositors," having for its object the protection and regulation of the wages of labour, agreeably to the Scale and acknowledged practices of the trade. The subscription was 4d. per month, the affairs of the Society being conducted by a Trade Council of twenty-four members, "who have worked as journeymen upwards of seven years in London," and who met every Tuesday evening at the "Red Lion," Red Lion Court, from 8.0 till 10.30, "the expenses of their refreshments not to exceed 6d. for each member present." On the first Tuesday evening in each month, the Council Meeting was open to every member of the Union, when the Minutes of the Proceedings of the Council during the preceding month were read.

The first Quarterly Meeting was held on the 1st of July; the report stating that "nearly 1,300 joined the Union on the first night of enrolment, 200 upon the second night," the then membership standing at 1,580. The Balance Sheet showed that £198 17s. 8½d. had been received during the quarter (including a gift of £55 from the General Trade Society); the expenditure amounting to £94 19s. 7½d., leaving the sum of £103 18s. 1d. in hand. From this period many important questions appear to have been referred to and dealt with by the Trade Council, including the charges for Appeal Cases (which resulted in the closing of Spottiswoode's), column matter in grammar and spelling books, running heads of a work when set in smaller type than the body of the work, the cast-up of the daily paper galley, and the right of the compositor to the wrapper of a work; also the apprentice and turnover system.

Among other matters dealt with was the question of relief to country compositors upon entering London, the Council deciding in 1834 that, as it had been announced that relief to London cards would be suspended unless corresponding relief was afforded to country cards, they had it in contemplation " to propose a plan by which immediate relief may be afforded to country compositors upon arrival in London."

Two resolutions were passed at the Second Delegate Meeting held in October of 1834, which are worthy of notice—the first declaring that a certain companionship was to insist upon charging the wrapper, without referring it to arbitration; and that, " in the event of the wrapper charge not being paid, the men on that work to leave, but that no other companionship be under the necessity of leaving the said house; and that the Trade Council use their best endeavours to prevent any person from applying for work at that house, till the wrapper in dispute be paid;" also " that 25s. per week be allowed to persons while out of employment, who have left their situations on disputed questions." It was further agreed that a levy of 1s. 6d. be made " to meet the present claims on the Union."

At the first Annual Meeting, held on February 2nd, 1835, it was reported that in addition to the sum of £245 8s. 1d. paid to members engaged in disputes, " the trade have voluntarily come forward to assist the Operative Builders in the struggle against their employers, and the sum of £65 10s., after deducting incidental expenses, was paid to them at a time when they stood much in need of every assistance that could be rendered." An effort was also made at this meeting to bring the newsmen into the Union, the members being invited to alter the rule governing the Saturday evening meeting to deal with news questions, whereby the number attending from the Council should be limited to the same number as the delegates from daily papers— " it having been intimated to the officers of the Union by members of the news trade that the fear of the number of the Council alone deterred the newsmen from joining the Union." Although the alteration of rule was approved, the object aimed at was not attained.

In the same year, the Trade Council appointed a Committee to inquire into "the present mode of working on 'The Times' and other newspapers," their Report— a most exhaustive one—with " Regulations for Casual Employment and Establishment Hours," being presented to and adopted by special general meetings held on the 15th and 23rd of September, 1835. At the second meeting a "Memorial of the Compositors of London to the Printer of 'The Times' Newspaper" was unanimously agreed to. An enquiry was also set on foot with the view of ascertaining "the number and nature of bastard founts in use in the business."

At the Tenth Quarterly Meeting the delegates had under consideration two most important matters—the first, a report dealing with the total failure of the efforts of the delegates appointed at the previous meeting "to effect an adjustment of the differences between the

Union and the members of the news trade;" also that of a Committee appointed by the News Council to "inquire into the mode of doing work by full hands on Weekly Papers." At the Annual Meeting a report was submitted from the two delegates appointed to represent the Union at a meeting of the Northern Union of the Typographical Association, held at Manchester; as well as a statement congratulating the trade upon the establishment of a relief fund for tramps.

In meeting the members at the Annual Meeting in 1837, a lengthy reference is made in the Council's report to the result of the Manchester meeting, notifying that societies had been established or re-organised in Ireland and Scotland, also in many towns in England (Brighton, Bristol, Oxford, and Cambridge); and that the Northern Union had been divided into four districts. Considerable reference is also made to the re-establishment, during the year, of the Association of Master Printers, "the Council knowing not whether they should call upon the trade to lament or to rejoice at this circumstance, since they are not aware whether the intentions of the Association be good or evil as regards the interests of those who work for them." At this meeting the Council proposed the establishment of a death payment of £20, to which an amendment was moved that £10 should be the sum the members voting being: For £20, 180; for £10, 140; against any allowance, 168. As the proposition was not supported by three-fourths of those present, the matter fell through.

At the fourth Annual Meeting of the Union, held in March, 1838, the report deals with the Parliamentary inquiry which had commenced into the constitution and methods of all Trade Unions (three members of the Council being appointed to give evidence before the Committee of Inquiry); whilst the Balance Sheet shows that loans of £50 each had been granted to the Curriers and to the Associated Typefounders' Society, and grants of £200 made to the Glasgow Compositors. The Council recommended (through a sub-committee) that its future meetings should be transferred from a public to a private house, urging that the fact of the Trade Council transacting its business in a public house "tends to undervalue their decisions in the opinions of those in whom we are most interested. 'Pot-house' decisions, it is well known, have been derided when they could not be impugned. The simple fact of our removal to a private building would be of more value as evidence of our moderation, our good sense, and our love of justice, than the most laboured disquisition could possibly effect. The meetings of delegates at present, in a crowded and ill-ventilated apartment, is a positive corporeal punishment, and any change must be acceptable to the gentlemen appointed to that office; besides, that the liquors drank during the discussion, and the noise created by publicans' servants, joined to the jingle of pots and glasses, must be alike injurious to the proper discharge of the duties with which they are entrusted, as they are known to be repugnant to the tastes of a large number of our members. . . The last class to which we would direct your attention is one which demands all your sympathy—that of the un-employed members. At present, to consult the registry, imperfect as it is, everyone must go to a public-house, where, for that slight accommodation, he feels bound to offer remuneration. This subjects him to pecuniary inconvenience; if he is without money he feels morally degraded in his own mind. To avoid this, he frequently pawns his labour in expectancy, and obtains that which, while it satisfies his sense of honour, renders him unfit for that labour he came to seek; when at length he does obtain it, the pledge has to be redeemed by abstracting from that which his family should partake, leaving them the victims of want — a living commentary on the erroneous course we have been pursuing."

The Council recommended that offices should be taken in Bouverie Street (No. 9½), Fleet Street, at a rental of 22 guineas per year; and that future Delegate Meetings should be held at the Royal British Schools, in Harp Alley, at a hiring fee of 8s. nightly; the expense of lighting (about 2s. 6d.) being borne by the Society. It was also agreed that, as it would be necessary to have a person in constant attendance during office hours, "in whom considerable trust would be vested," the officers of registrar, assistant-registrar, and office-keeper should be held by one member at a salary of 36s. per week; "but in the event of a junction of the News Department with this Union, a secretary to that body must be retained, whose salary will then be determined." The office-keeper's duties were to "open and close the rooms, keep lists of men and situations, receive and pay money for petitions," etc. It is interesting to note that in the report read to the members it was stated that "books can be printed in a foreign land and sold in England at a cheaper rate than we can print them." At this meeting a former member made personal application to be re-admitted to membership, and a resolution was passed " that the applicant having thrown himself on the mercy of this meeting, he be permitted to join the London Union of Compositors."

At the Annual Meeting held on July 9th, 1839, considerable reference was made to the newly-formed Masters' Association, which those outside the Union were apparently holding it responsible for bringing into existence. During the year the trade was so greatly depressed that a Relief Committee was appointed to raise subscriptions on behalf of the unemployed, the amount realised being £112, of which £92 was distributed to members holding the previous year's card; and £20, subscribed by newspaper compositors unconnected with the Union, to those who had not cards, or who were not members of the Union. The report also states that with regard to the News Department, the Trade Council had made arrangements whereby forty additional members had been added to the Union, " thus giving to us a majority in the News Trade." The collapse of the Parliamentary inquiry into Trade Unions is noted; as well as the endeavour of the Union to carry into effect its seventh Article, by establishing a Council of Arbitration composed of an equal number of masters and journeymen, " to which all disputes might be referred, and whose decisions should be binding upon both parties," regret being expressed at the refusal of the employers to favourably entertain the proposal. Reference is also made to a circular issued by the employers, some months after their refusal to meet the men in arbitration, questioning the compositors' right to the wrappers and advertising sheets of magazines, reviews, etc. After Delegate and Special General Meetings had considered the question, a Memorial was presented by deputation to the Masters' Association on January 11th, 1839, and an agreement arrived at.

At a later period of the year a second Memorial was presented, asking for an increase of $\frac{1}{4}d.$ per thousand upon magazine work, and dealing with the question of reprints and leaded matter—in all, seven propositions being submitted. The reply of the Masters' Committee being of an unsatisfactory character, it was arranged that a deputation should attend before the masters' representatives; but upon presenting themselves at Anderton's Hotel upon the agreed-upon date (June 20th) they were informed that in consequence of a dispute having arisen in an office regarding the charging of a wrapper (a matter dealt with and settled earlier in the year), which the men refused to submit to the decision of the Masters' Committee, the latter declined to receive the deputation, thereby breaking off the negotiations.

The report of this year is also noticeable as containing a suggestion that the time had arrived when the members might well consider the propriety and advisability of providing certain contingent benefits, experience having proved that in course of time purely trade societies "languish and decay." The Balance Sheet showed that £52 17s. 6d. remained in the Treasurer's hands at the close of the year.

For the following year the report dealt largely with the amounts distributed by the Relief Committee to unemployed members, the task proving to be a delicate and disagreeable one, the Committee stating that "to relieve misfortune, and not to punish folly," was the object for which they had been appointed, but that they "would ill perform their duty to the trade did they not state, after exercising the utmost vigilance, several cases were relieved which were not perhaps strictly worthy of the bounty of the trade;" the Committee concluding their report by urging "that while there will always be many ready to avail themselves of pecuniary relief, it will but seldom be received by those who really need or deserve it," and advising the members to discontinue the practice of raising funds for such a purpose.

Another subject discussed was that of appointing delegates to attend the meeting of the Northern Union, at which the apprentice question was to be dealt with, a return having been prepared showing that in London there were 534 apprentices employed to 1,343 journeymen, the report stating that, allowing for the offices from which no returns had been received, the number of apprentices "must be nearly 700," and suggesting that an immediate effort should be made to limit the number to one in four.

In the following year the Annual Meeting did not take place, a Special General Meeting having been held in the month of April, causing the Trade Council to consider it unnecessary "to still further increase the heavy expenses of the year" by convening the annual gathering. Therefore, the meeting assembled in the theatre of the London Mechanics' Institution on April 11th, 1842, was called to receive the " Report of the

Trade Council for the years 1840 and 1841." The attention of the members was drawn mainly to the question of finance, three general meetings and nine delegated meetings having been held during the previous year, "there having been no period since the establishment of the Union in which so many disputes and such frequent subjects of litigation had arisen." During the two years the sum of £125 had been expended in relief to persons visiting London in search of employment, " a sum far exceeding what was anticipated when, at the urgent request of the country societies, a tramp relief fund was established in connection with the London Union." Reference having been made to the increased expense of management consequent upon the renting of private premises for conducting the Society's business, it was decided by the meeting to revert to the former practice of holding the meetings in a public house. It was also stated that only 1,000 members contributed regularly to the Union.

At the Annual Meeting held in 1843, a report was presented by the delegates attending the meeting of the Northern Union, held in Leeds during the preceding year, in which reference was made to the following proposition, which had been unanimously agreed upon :—
"That a General Tramping Reimbursement Fund be established, comprising the societies of the Northern Union and the London Compositors' and Pressmen's Unions, and that the money raised be placed under the control of the Committee of Management of the Northern Union; that the amount of contribution towards such Reimbursement Fund be one penny per

month from the members of the Northern Union (in addition to the sum of ninepence per month as at present paid by them for the relief of tramps, into the funds of the societies), and twopence per month from the members of the London Compositors' and Pressmen's Unions." The Trade Council advised the adoption of these propositions, but the delegates disagreed, although prepared to pay the Northern Union the difference between the amounts paid by their societies to the London men and that paid to their members by the London Union. With the report of the meeting is embodied the "Rules and Regulations for the Government of the Northern Typographical Union, adopted at a Meeting of Delegates held in Leeds on the 6th, 7th, 8th and 9th days of June, 1842," which, as stated above, was attended by two delegates from the London Union, and one from the Pressmen's Union, each of whom had been instructed by the delegates of their respective societies to support the establishment of a fund for relieving tramps.

For some long period prior to the holding of this meeting, a strong disposition had been manifested on the part of the Trade Council to make an effort to establish branches outside London, and in the report issued in 1837, particular attention is drawn to an alteration which had been made in the Rules dealing with "the incorporation of country societies," which read as follows :—" That compositors in country towns desirous of uniting themselves to the London Society of Compositors, may constitute an Association in their respective towns, nominating a Secretary to correspond with the Registrar of the London Union." These local associations were to be allowed the power of settling minor disputes with employers, but were not permitted to deal with the question of the rates of wages or the hours of labour, or with the closing of any house, without the sanction of the Trade Council of the London Union. The practical outcome of the desire and intention to extend the sphere of the Union's operations is not quite clear; but there is abundant evidence to prove that during times of dispute men would come from the provinces to London, or *vice versâ*—in the majority of cases unknowingly—to take the places of men who had sacrificed their situations upon principle, the feeling thereby engendered stimulating the desire that some closer bond of union should be brought about between the various societies throughout the Kingdom.

Apparently, in 1844, effect was given to this long-desired understanding, as on the 10th of September of that year a General Meeting of the Compositors of London was convened at the Mechanics' Institution, to receive a "Report of the National Typographical Association." This report claimed that the proposed association was merely an extension, or carrying out, of the principles which, for fourteen years in the North, and for ten years in London, had been acted upon; the "only really important difference being, in the first place, that instead of, as hitherto, giving partial and casual relief to the unemployed, a permanent allowance of 6s. per week will be given; and, in the second, the establishment of a different system of co-operation—of the merits of which every individual must form his own opinion." After stating that two years' deliberations had been devoted to maturing the plan, which was "founded upon a practical experience of the errors of the present system, and a conviction, occasioned by a defeat after a long and severe struggle, that the present operations of our respective unions are incapable of working any real good, either in retarding the introduction of apprentices or in defending the prices of labour," the report goes on to state that, whatever the decision of that meeting, "things cannot, and will not, remain as they are. The time for a change has arrived, and it is not in the power of the London trade to postpone it. The societies in the North have declared the operations of their Union to be ineffective. . . . and having framed regulations for a new and a different system, to come into operation on January 1st next; unless that change be accompanied by a corresponding alteration here, our unemployed will be prevented from receiving relief while travelling, while it will not prevent persons in the provinces receiving relief while on their way to London."

After giving a lengthy and exhaustive explanation of the objects of the proposed association, the Trade Council urge as prospective advantages to the London trade that "the number of hands poured into it by strikes and partial interruption of employment in country towns will be diminished, and a more ample and certain provision made for its unemployed members." With reference to the first advantage, the grounds for such belief were that, in the provinces, "half-a-dozen, or even a less number of individuals, have hitherto had the power of closing houses and sending adrift upon the trade whomsoever they pleased. We need not stop to inquire whether the power has been wisely or unwisely exercised; but the power has been used by the Northern Union, and to such an extent that there is scarcely a town within its limits that does not contain two or three closed houses. In only fourteen towns in the Northern Union there are no less than fifty-three prohibited or unfair offices."

The result was that the members gave their adhesion to the establishment of the National Typographical Association, which was divided into five districts—the South-Eastern (embodying London), South-Western, Midland, Western (comprising all Ireland), and the Northern (comprising all Scotland). Each district had a separate Board, consisting of nine members, meeting within the first seven days of each month, and holding office for one year. On the 16th of April, 1845, a meeting was held in the Harp Alley Schoolroom, Harp Alley, Farringdon Street, at which was read "the First Quarterly Report of the Committee of the London Society of Compositors, in connection with the National Typographical Association (South-Eastern District)." The report stated that the number of members joining the London section of the new Society to the 5th of April was 1,751, of whom 657 were clear with the London Union and other societies, 214 were less than twelve months in arrear to the London Union, and 880 had been admitted upon payment of an entry fee of 5s. In this statement was included 140 who had entered the News Department of the Society, 125 of whom were clear with the old Society, and fifteen new members. Out of this 140 there were 120 employed upon daily newspapers, "which argues much against the usefulness of the Society that still is estranged from us—'the Society of London Daily Newspaper Compositors.'" A strong appeal to the newsmen was embodied in the report, "their cause being ours," and urging upon them that "if they would only do their duty, they would at once become a part and parcel of this Society, and make it, as a society of compositors, perfect." The necessity of perseverance and insistence upon the collection and payment of subscriptions was duly pointed out, so that the "system of arrears" might be uprooted—"a system which has lost many a good man to the Society;" members being advised to cherish the principle that "the man who cannot pay one week can less afford to pay two, and certainly not three or four;" the report concluding by inviting cordial support to the new Association, by the establishment of which "the London trade has assumed a position powerful in its bearing and honourable to themselves."

At a later period (May 25th) a Special Delegate Meeting was held at which the "Bye-laws of the London Society of Compositors" were agreed to, a graduated scale of subscription being adopted—members earning 33*s*. or upwards paying 6*d*. per week; 22*s*. and less than 33*s*., 4*d*.; 16*s*. 6*d*. and less than 22*s*., 3*d*.; 11*s*. and less than 10*s*. 6*d*., 2*d*.; under 11*s*. no subscription being required. With this exception the Rules under which the business of the London Union had hitherto been conducted remained practically unaltered.

From the first Half-yearly Report of the National Typographical Association (January 1st to June 30th) issued in August, 1845, it is gathered that the progress of the Association in the South-Eastern District was regarded as being "highly satisfactory." Besides London, branches existed in Oxford, Cambridge (both for Compositors and Pressmen), Aylesbury, and Hertford. The membership was 4,320, of which the South-Eastern District claimed 2,000, the Western (Ireland) District 569, the Northern (Scotland) District 800, and the Midland and South-Western Districts 714 and 237 respectively. Of the total income of the Association (£1,637 17s. 8½d.), the South-Eastern District contributed £701 3s. 9d., the expenditure, however, amounting to £485 4s. 6d., the total expenditure of the Association for the six months amounting to £713 17s. 1d.

Two items of interest were mentioned in the report of the Secretary of the South-Eastern District—First, that the Executive of the Association had been asked: "Will you support the London trade in maintaining the price of 8d. per 1,000 for Appeal Cases, in opposition to the declaration of the masters?" whose proposal was to pay but 7d. per thousand for such work. Secondly, the right of a compositor to recover a fortnight's wages in lieu of notice. Circumstances took both questions into a Court of Law, and, although the Chief Baron of the Court of Exchequer gave it as his opinion that the decision of his Court would be of no value to the plaintiffs, since the Court could not compel the masters to pay, nor the journeyman to receive, a certain price for any description of work, yet (the report states) the legal proceedings were attended with some advantage, having secured an "unqualified acknowledgment" of the right of the journeymen to a fortnight's notice, and afforded the trade an opportunity of proving, beyond the possibility of dispute, that the practice of the London trade for a series of years in charging Appeal Cases has been 8*d.* per thousand.

The report of the South-Eastern District Board for the second half-year (December 25th, 1845) states that unsuccessful efforts had been made to establish branches at Dover, Maidstone and Bedford; but success had attended similar efforts in Woking, Lewes and Brighton, the total membership (of nine branches) being 2,367, of which London claimed 2,200. At the end of the year the total membership of the Association was 4,971; and the income £3,385 8*s.* 1½*d.*, towards which the South-Eastern District contributed £1,317 19*s.* 11*d.* (less an expenditure of £312 4*s.* 7*d.*)

During the first half of the year 1846 the Delegate Meeting of the Association was held in London, when several of the Rules were altered and a uniform system of keeping the accounts agreed upon. Of the 2,510 members embraced in the South-Eastern District (comprising ten branches), 2,350 belonged to the London Branch; the membership of the Association at this period numbering 5,421.

Reference is made in the Fourth Half-Yearly Report (issued in March, 1847) to the necessity that had arisen for doubling the subscription—mainly in consequence of the number of members unemployed, and the large number of disputes (over ninety) referred to the Executive for adjudication. As a result of the heavy outlay, and in spite of the increased subscription, the funds of the Association had been seriously reduced, and it was decided that the levy should run for a further period of three months. The report of the South-Eastern District Board refers to the "trying character" of the vicissitudes to which this branch of the Association had been exposed; and states that from a sudden and unprecedented dearth of employment—especially in London —the "enormous sum of £1,200" had been expended in unemployed relief—consequent upon a rumour gaining currency in the provinces that unusual activity prevailed in the London trade, and that "great sums" were being earned by the compositors. The result was that "journeymen poured in from almost every part of the empire"—in many cases homes being broken up, and the families brought to the Metropolis. The "deep suffering" which ensued would, it was hoped, prove a warning to members, especially as it was one of the objects of the Association "to prevent this useless and painful migration of labour." Of the district membership of 2,417, 2,200 were in the London Branch; the total number of members in the Association at this period being 5,418. The receipts of the five districts for the six months amounted to £1,561 2s. 9d. and the expenditure to £2,400 3s. 0½d., the funds of the Association being reduced from £1,241 6s. 8d. (end of June) to £402 6s. 4½d. (December 31st, 1846).

Both the District and the Executive reports refer to the extreme difficulties, arising from unforeseen and adverse circumstances, which had overtaken the Association, "which the enemies of our interests have not failed to turn to our disadvantage;" and in a special circular issued by the South-Eastern Board, and signed by the Treasurer (J. Catchpool) and Secretary (R. Thompson), it is stated "that if ever there was a period at which the manifestation of zeal, alacrity and determination on the part of the trade was required," it was then; reference also being made to the number of members who had been called upon to "sacrifice permanent and lucrative situations," and to the unemployed, who had "resisted the lures of the underworking employer, and had chosen rather to struggle with necessity than sacrifice the interests of their brethren."

It is apparent, however, that at this period the affairs of the Association were in a far from satisfactory condition, and at a numerously-attended Special General Meeting of the members of the London Society, held at the Mechanics' Institution, on September 2nd, 1847, four resolutions were submitted, the most important being "That the amended laws of the National Typographical Association be printed, and with them a Voting Paper, whereby the members may each individually record their opinions as to the propriety of the London trade continuing to be a Branch of the said Association, under the amended laws." Having been adopted by the meeting, a Ballot Paper was accordingly issued, signed by the President (J. Atkinson) and Secretary (E. Edwards), and the vote resulted as follows: For the continuance of the Association, 746; against, 468; majority in favour, 278. The result was announced to the members at a Special General Meeting, held at the National Hall, High Holborn, on the 15th September, at which a statement was submitted by the

Committee, strongly urging upon the minority the necessity of falling in with the decision of the majority, and pointing out that unless a proper understanding was arrived at upon certain propositions, " the great expense the Society is now subject to must be stopped, as the strike and unemployed hands could no longer be paid."

At the Eleventh Quarterly Delegate Meeting, held at the Farringdon Hall, King's Arms Yard, Snow Hill, on October 20th, 1847, in addition to the ordinary business, the whole question was again raised, the newly-appointed District Committee having issued a strongly-worded circular "to those individuals who, during the last few months, have suspended their payments to the London Branch of the National Typographical Association."

On the 2nd of November, a Special General Meeting was convened at the Mechanics' Institution, Southampton Buildings, "for the purpose of considering the exigencies of the Society, and devising means to discharge the liabilities of the Association." The Committee recommended the members to agree to the operation of Rules 35 and 40, " so far as regards payment of moneys " being suspended, " until such time as the said debts are wholly cleared," and that during this suspension the subscription of each Society should be divided into a weekly dividend, according to the amount received, and paid to those persons to whom the Society was indebted, " as part payment of the sum due." Members falling out of work to be included in the dividend ; " but no arrears to be considered as due to the member, consequent upon his receiving less than the sum stated in the Rules."

On the 10th of November, a General Meeting of the "Compositors of London" was held in the same Institution, "to hear the report of the journeymen appointed in June last to serve as an Arbitration Committee, in pursuance of a resolution previously agreed to, viz., 'That a Committee composed of eight masters and eight journeymen be formed, for the purpose of finally determining all matters not touched upon or clearly defined in the Scale of 1805-10.'" Admission to the meeting was given "to all persons stating to the doorkeepers that they were compositors."

A Circular was issued by the District Committee of the Society, on the 17th December, 1847, notifying that on and after the 1st of January, 1848, the subscription would be reduced to 2d. for members earning 8s. and less than 12s., increasing 1d. for every additional 4s. earned, up to a maximum payment of 8d. per week. A note is appended to the Circular, requesting "those persons to whom the Society is indebted, and who have not yet applied for payment, to do so forthwith, so that their accounts may be liquidated in common with those which since November have been, and continue to be, discharged weekly."

On the 19th of January, 1848, the Twelfth Quarterly Delegate Meeting of the Association was held in the Farringdon Hall, Snow Hill, for the purpose, amongst other matters, of receiving a statement (addressed to the Members of the London Society of Compositors) from the District Committee, "explanatory of certain propositions which, at the forthcoming Annual Meeting of the Society, they intend to place before the members in relation to the Association and the requirements of the London Trade." In this address to the delegates, the District Committee, at considerable length, gave their reasons for advising the trade to break away from the National Association, and to form a separate Society for London. They pointed out that whereas the Association was formerly the Union of the many— it was now the hope only of the few. Starting operations in a year (1845) when trade was unusually active, the prospect of success seemed bright; but when activity was succeeded by dearth of work and derangement, and dispute followed dispute, discontent, ill-feeling, and secession followed. "Disappointed and litigious men had commenced, and were now more fully intent upon carrying on, the work of destruction;" and by withholding their own support when it was most needed, and embittering the minds of others far more consistent, "yet equally susceptible to false impressions on themselves, these men have succeeded in impairing the efficiency of the Association." With regard to London, the largest of the sixty-five branches, the receipts had fallen to about a third of what they formerly were, "700 men not having paid a fraction towards the Union for many months past." Dublin had ceased to be a branch of the Association; Liverpool had but one-half of its former membership; and Edinburgh only fifty paying members, many of the smaller societies having entirely seceded.

Believing, therefore, that the London Society would progress better if freed from those situate elsewhere, and having ascertained, after watching assiduously the proceedings of the Association during the last four months,

" and observing that the several societies are not content even to obey the laws of the executive body," the Committee advised a dissolution, and submitted a resolution in these terms :

"That in consequence of the numerous secessions which have taken place both in town and country from the ranks of the National Typographical Association, and also the continued indifference exhibited on its behalf, this Branch deems it necessary, for the maintenance of union, to cease connection with the afore-named Association, forming in its place a local society apart from, but in friendly connection with, all other typographical societies in the three kingdoms."

At the Third Annual General Meeting of the London Branch of the National Typographical Association, held at the Mechanics' Institution, on February 1st, 1848, the above resolution was unanimously endorsed, and in addition the following :

"That this meeting hereby establishes a local trade society, to be called The London Society of Compositors, for the purpose of protecting and regulating the wages of labour, agreeably to the provisions contained in the London Scale of Prices (as agreed to by a Conference of Masters and Compositors in 1847); as also the Scale of Prices regulating News and Parliamentary Work ; together with such customs and usages as belong to the profession, not directly mentioned in the Scales above alluded to."

The subscriptions were reduced to 2*d*. per week for members earning less than 20*s*.; less than 30*s*., 3*d*.; over that sum, 4*d*.; no subscriptions being paid by members earning less than 15*s*.

It was also decided to establish a Provident Fund upon the voluntary principle, the Committee being empowered to pay into such fund one-fourth of the actual sums received quarterly in both book and news departments of the Society, the sum thus paid not to exceed £200 per year. In order that this Voluntary Provident Fund might be established, a general meeting of compositors favourable to its formation was specially convened, at which the benefit was fixed at 8*s*. per week for a period of fifteen weeks, the subscription being 2*d*. per week.

At a Special General Meeting held at the Mechanics' Institute on the 29th of February, the Rules for the government of the Trade Society were agreed upon, and likewise Rules for the "London Compositors' Provident Fund;" the contribution to which was fixed at 2*d*. per week, securing to the member, after six months' membership, the payment of £6 annually (£3 in each half-year).

During the month of March, 1848, a General Meeting of the Society of London Daily Newspaper Compositors was held, and a report presented in which reference was made to the two unsuccessful attempts which had been made to bring about a good understanding between its members and those engaged in the book department - the first emanating from the latter body three years previously, the second from a committee appointed by the newsmen. Reference is also made to the fact that, although the Society contained less than 200 members, they had subscribed upwards of £420 to assist the Edinburgh compositors in their struggle with the employers, which ultimately proved successful.

From the annual statement for 1847 of the South-Eastern District of the National Typographical Association, the sum of £766 8s. is set forth as having been subscribed by the bookmen towards the support of their fellow workmen in Scotland.

LONDON SOCIETY OF COMPOSITORS.

Re-established January, 1848.

The first noteworthy business engaging the attention of the members was a proposition submitted to the newly-established Society by the Masters' Association, suggesting that a Committee of Reference should be appointed, consisting of twelve master printers, of not less than five years' standing in the business, six to be chosen by the masters, and six by the compositors. This proposal was considered at the first Quarterly Delegate Meeting, held on the 12th of April, and amended in the direction of appointing a mixed Committee of masters and journeymen (which the delegates, agreeing with the principle, believed to be the only fair and equitable method of appointing such Committee); the Secretary of the Masters' Association, in reply, intimating that "the proposition is one which the masters feel they cannot accede to, or even entertain," and advising the men to "seriously re-consider the question." The report stated that the Society had a membership of 1,200, of whom 300 subscribed to the Provident Fund; and that during the quarter the amounts due to strike hands and unemployed members at the commencement of the year (£215) had been fully paid.

On the 1st of June a circular was addressed to the Compositors of London, announcing that the National Typographical Association had been re-modelled, and inviting Compositors to join the London Trade Society of Compositors, held at the "Green Dragon," Fleet Street, which claimed to have enrolled upwards of 200 members since its establishment on the 1st of January. The entry fee up to July 1st was 6d.; after that date 2s., the circular being signed by R. Matthews, Secretary.

Later in the month (on Saturday, the 24th), a General Meeting of the News Department of the London Society was held at the "Falcon" Tavern, Gough Square, at which a series of propositions were submitted for discussion, "to be appended to the Rules of the Society." These Rules were agreed to, by which a Committee (consisting of a delegate from each morning and evening newspaper, and a delegate from each weekly or other newspaper, with two members of the Book Committee) was appointed to deal with questions connected with newspapers, meeting on the first Saturday evening in each month, each Committeeman present being allowed 1s. "as remuneration to the landlord."

The Rules also provided that in the event of a dispute arising in any daily newspaper office, which it was deemed necessary should be sent before the trade for adjudication, the delegates from the Daily Newspaper Society, with those of the News Branch of the London Society, should meet together for the discusssion and settlement of the same, at an hour and place appointed by the Secretaries of the two Societies.

The second Quarterly Meeting was held at the Caxton Institution, Nevils' Court, Fetter Lane, the statement of accounts embodying the receipts and expenditure of the News Department; and setting forth that sixty-seven tramps (at 5s. each) had been relieved by the Society, whereas but fifty London members had been relieved by country societies. It was also noted that 370 members belonged to the Provident Fund. Naturally, the working of these two benefits was very closely watched, particularly the former, frequent references being made to the fact that for every London member relieved by country societies, two provincial members were relieved by the London Society. During the first year, 144 country cards were relieved, at an expenditure of £36; and during 1849 this item amounted to £51 5s. (204 at 5s. and two at 2s. 6d. each), whereas in the following year 173 members were relieved at an expenditure of £43 5s.

At this meeting an appeal was made to the London trade to render pecuniary assistance to certain individuals (connected with the Northern District Board) who, during the strike in Edinburgh in the preceding year, had made themselves responsible for money borrowed for and on behalf of the Edinburgh Society, with the approval of the Executive of the late Association, and were being pressed for payment, the delegates deciding to open a voluntary subscription towards defraying a portion of this liability.

At the succeeding Quarterly Meeting a proposal was submitted (which, however, failed to find favour) that, in order to secure a more regular and larger attendance of delegates, the Society should pay 1s. from the funds to each delegate in attendance at the commencement of business. A circular was also issued drawing attention to an irregularity in the manner of engaging members upon weekly papers, who, in many instances, were working for two or three days at a 'stab rate of 6s. per day, instead of on time at 10d. per hour, or on the piece— the only systems recognised for men engaged for less than a week.

Towards the close of the year 1848 the Committee issued a circular to offices and individuals unconnected with the Society, drawing attention to the advantages attaching to membership, and to the resistance which had been offered during the short time the Society had been re-constituted to encroachments upon the Scale or customs of the trade, which, had they not been resisted, would have had a serious effect upon the prosperity of the profession at large. At this period the membership was 1,200, of whom 200 did not contribute to the funds on account of being unemployed or earning less than 15s. per week.

On the 20th of December, the first Annual General Meeting of the Provident Fund was held, at which it was proposed that, on account of the dearth of trade, the benefit should be temporarily fixed at £4 per year (instead of £6, as per Rule); the Committee inviting members to invest them with power to exclude those detected in imposing upon the fund, giving the excluded member the right to appeal to the general meeting; and strenuously urging the necessity for all members to belong to the fund, "as an appreciation on the part of the majority of the trade of the integrity of those individuals who endure sacrifices rather than endanger the trade rules and prices."

In the printed report for the Fourth Quarterly Meeting, held on January 17th, 1849, it was proposed that as the proprietors of two offices had "given their word as gentlemen, that the prices and regulations of the trade shall be by them, in future, observed," their offices should be declared "fair" to the members of the Society, the particulars of the disputes, and "the means by which the wished-for alteration has been effected," being set forth in the written report read to the delegates.

The first Annual General Meeting was held at the Harp Alley Schoolroom, on February 7th, 1849, when, in addition to the election of Secretary and Treasurer, and the nomination of six Stockholders, the following was set down for discussion: "To consider a statement to be made by a deputation from the London department of the Sheffield Trades' Committee, respecting the prosecution of Messrs. Drury (Secretary), Bullos, Marsden and Hall (members of Committee), for—as alleged—inciting two persons, brothers, named Heathcoats (members of the Sheffield Razor Grinders' Union), to destroy machinery at Sheffield;" and to resolve, "Whether or not a sum of money shall be voted from the funds, or a voluntary subscription be entered into, on behalf of the indicted, to enable them to meet by counsel and proper legal advice, the charge mentioned, at the ensuing Spring Assizes." The Heathcoats were first charged with destroying machinery, and sentenced to three months' imprisonment. Before this they were drawing unemployed benefit; and upon leaving prison immediately declared upon the funds; the Secretary and Committee refusing to recognise their claim, "both having been well known as of dissolute habits, and as unceasing recipients of the Society's funds." For the second offence they were sentenced to seven years' transportation, and previous to leaving the country they were seen by an official of the Sheffield Manufacturers' Protection Association, after which the above-mentioned officials of the union were charged with "inciting, moving, and stirring up Alexander and Thomas Heathcoats to destroy certain machinery."

The trial of the Secretary and members of the Committee took place at the York Spring Assizes in 1848, and upon the evidence given by the convicts they were sentenced to ten years' transportation. The judge having committed an error in passing sentence, the judgment was reversed, and the accused liberated; but a fresh indictment was immediately preferred against them, to be pleaded to at the following Spring Assizes, and it was at this moment that the appeal for financial assistance was made to the Society, the members voting the sum of £20.

In May of 1849 a General Meeting of master printers, newspaper proprietors, compositors, pressmen, machinists, etc., presided over by Mr. L. J. Hansard, was held at the Mechanics' Institution, at which Mr. E. Edwards, the Secretary of the Society, read a most interesting paper upon the "Duties on Paper, Advertisements, and Newspapers," and the particularly injurious effect which these fiscal exactions had upon the printing trade.

This was followed by the Committee placing before the delegates, at the Fifth Quarterly Meeting, a proposal that a General Meeting of the Letterpress Printers of London should be convened for the purpose of discussing the propriety of petitioning Parliament to repeal the duties upon paper and advertisements, as well as the penny stamp duty on newspapers; and on the 22nd of May, Mr. Hansard presided over a meeting, held at the same Institution, at which a petition to Parliament was submitted for consideration, and its terms unanimously endorsed.

During the same month a Special Delegate Meeting was held to consider an invitation received from the Liverpool Society, that delegates might be appointed to attend a meeting to be held at Sheffield, for the purpose of establishing a provincial union, " similar in character to the late Northern Union," one of the principal matters to be discussed being the important question of tramping. Two delegates were appointed by the Meeting to watch the proceedings, advise and co-operate with their fellow delegates, " but in no way pledging the London Society to adopt any particular principle, the members not having been consulted thereon."

As a result of this meeting a proposition was placed before the members of the Provincial Typographical Association, whereby the system of tramp relief might be abolished, and a " well-digested" scheme of emigration substituted in its place ; and, at the Sixth Quarterly Meeting, a scheme was submitted for the establishment of a self-sustaining Emigration Fund, the subscription to be 2*d*. per week, securing a grant of £10 " to those of the subscribers who shall be elected by ballot every half-year." From the half-yearly report of the Provident Fund, presented at this meeting, it was stated that eighty-one members had been relieved, twenty of whom had drawn the maximum benefit—the Committee hoping that in the following year they would be able to increase the payments to £5 per year—perhaps £6.

On the 3rd of October the Committee convened a Special Delegate Meeting to receive a deputation from a Committee connected with the Bookbinders' trade, respecting the position of the bookfolders and sewers recently employed by the Contractors to the British and Foreign Bible Society, who, to the number of 153, were out on strike, "as it is commonly termed," to obtain "that requital for their labour which was being paid by all employers who bind for the Christian Knowledge Society," etc. In addition to low wages, an elaborate system of fines was imposed upon the girls, and the delegates decided to grant towards their support the sum of £30, and to open a voluntary subscription, the dispute having lasted for several weeks.

The Circular convening the meeting refers to a proposition then before the trade of the three kingdoms, to raise a sum of money for the purpose of obtaining two prize addresses on the subject of Apprentices—one address to be dedicated to the employers, the other to the journeymen.

At the next Quarterly Meeting the Committee were called upon to state "Who ought to contribute to the Society," and replied: "Those who work at case, or who have to do with case, directly or indirectly, ought to subscribe to maintain the prices of case-work." Readers and overseers, it was agreed, might justifiably plead exemption; but, if disposed to pay by virtue of having been a compositor, "the Society's laws do not oblige the officers to refuse his subscriptions." Strong representations were made upon the subject of "turnovers," and in order to prevent boys from going about the trade unrestrictedly, chapels were urged to insist that such lads should be bound for a definite period, emphasis being laid upon the fact that unless this was done considerable difficulty would be experienced in gaining admission to the Society.

Attention was also drawn to the number of "rafflepapers" and petitions which members were being called upon to relieve, many of them issued on behalf of men who had never belonged to the trade society, chapels being advised to adopt a rule refusing recognition to petitions not bearing the Secretary's signature, "in order to secure to the trade that respect for forethought and charity which particular chapels at the present time enjoy."

In presenting the eighth Quarterly Report, the Committee referred to the fact (as evidence of the "increasing greatness" of the Society) that the subscriptions for the three months had amounted to £203— a sum which the promoters of the Society two years ago confidently hoped to see contributed—viz., £800 per year. The report notes that of 400 members belonging to the Provident Society, 100 had been pecuniarily assisted; and, with regard to strike benefits, recommended the adoption of a graduated scale of payments.

The Annual Report of the Provident Society for 1849 mentions the expulsion of a member through drawing benefit whilst earning from 18s. to 30s. per week; and also refers to two other cases arising from a misconception of the words "earning" and "received," in consequence of the existence of the practice known as "horse." The definition of the word "earning" was given as the amount received, whether on account or for work performed, those only being eligible to the benefits of the fund who were solely dependent upon it for the aid afforded. Members were invited to join the fund, the Committee, as an example, citing the fact that it included the names of very many men holding, "to all external appearances," lasting situations upon daily papers, from offices furnishing eighty members, or one-fifth of the whole number.

The Second Annual Meeting of the Society was held in February, 1850, only formal business being transacted; but on March 12th, a Special General Meeting was held to consider a letter from Mr. Edwards, the Secretary, resigning the position to which he had been re-elected six weeks previously, and which he had held for four years prior to the Society being re-established. The Committee made an unsuccessful effort to retain the services of Mr. Edwards (who had obtained an appointment in the office in which he had formerly worked as a journeyman), and the members regretfully accepted their Secretary's resignation.

There were six candidates for the vacant position, five of whom went to the poll, the choice of the members falling upon Mr. J. Boyett, of Gilbert and

Rivington's, who polled 731 votes, against 348 given to Mr. W. Millar, of Barclay's. Out of 1,351 members entitled to vote, 1,135 exercised their right. The newly-appointed Secretary took office on the 1st of May.

As a final settlement on the part of the London trade of the debts incurred in connection with the late Association in Edinburgh, the delegates in April voted a further sum of £20.

About this period there is evidence that an understanding was likely to be brought about between the Society and the Daily Newspaper Compositors' Society, a Joint Committee, representative of the latter and of the News Department being appointed to inquire into the system of employing assistants on the first editions of evening papers, who reported to a General Meeting during the month of April, when the half-galley charge was agreed upon.

For some time, only routine business engaged the attention of the delegates, but at the meeting in April of 1851, applications for financial assistance were considered from the Manchester and Cork Societies—in the first instance, a dispute arising through the introduction of female and boy labour at case, the proprietors claiming a perfect right "to do what they liked with their own;" and in the second, the whole of the "'ship" sacrificing their situations in consequence of the refusal of the employer to pay night-money to men "called out of their beds at two in the morning" to assist in producing an extraordinary edition of the paper, containing the Queen's Speech; and on another occasion being "gathered from their various places of Sabbath resort or worship" for a similar purpose. To the Manchester Society £20, and to the Cork Society £50, were unanimously voted. At the following meeting a grant of £50 was made to the Tinplate Workers' Society, six of whose members had been committed for trial on a charge of conspiracy.

An appeal for voluntary subscriptions was also issued to the trade at the close of the year on behalf of the Paris compositors, many hundreds of whom had been thrown out of employment through the suppression of most of the daily and weekly newspapers, the Committee reporting that although it was often remarked that it was their "duty to look at home," they relied upon the spirit of liberality which had hitherto characterised the acts of the London printers, and deemed it unnecessary to attempt "a refutation of this peculiarly selfish doctrine."

In January of 1852, the News Department presented an important report to the members attending the Annual Meeting, giving a detailed statement of the steps which had been taken in the direction of bringing about an amalgamation—the daily paper hands (numbering less than 600) being divided into three sections. The Joint Committee previously referred to had been appointed in agreement with certain resolutions passed by the chapel of an office in which members of the Daily News Society were largely employed; and although the attempt to amalgamate was not for the moment successful, the Committee were hopeful that it was but a question of time when so desirable and necessary a consummation would be brought about.

In agreement with the practice then prevailing, a Special General Meeting was convened on February 11th, 1852, to receive a deputation in support of an application from the Amalgamated Society of Engineers for pecuniary help, to whom the sum of £100 was granted - representing nearly one-third of the Society's total income during the preceding quarter.

Rules preventing members contracting, by way of farming, to do any description of jobbing or book work, or accepting engagements on any such work so contracted for, and stipulating that, in future, no money should be voted by the delegates unless due notice had been placed upon the Business Paper, were discussed at the April Delegate Meeting; and at the following meeting a proposal was submitted that "the Cards of the Daily News Society be exchanged free, as in the case of provincial societies."

In September a circular was issued by Mr. A. Mason, Secretary of the "Compositors' Emigration Aid Society," announcing that active work had commenced, members having been enrolled from the different societies, the weekly subscription being fixed at 3d. (no entrance fee).

Steady and continuous progress appears to have been made by the Trade Society, each quarter showing an increase in its funds, which, in the annual statement for 1852, amounted to £1,862 15s. 5d.

From a circular issued in November, 1852, it appeared that a serious dispute had arisen in one of the daily paper offices, from which several members had been "evicted" on the 16th of October, to make room for men who had "engaged to work on a system in direct opposition to the London Scale," a Defence Committee being appointed by the Society, who immediately approached the independent society with the object of securing combined action, resulting in a joint committee being formed on the 6th of November. Deputations were sent to the various trade organisations, inviting financial assistance; and also to the principal licensed victuallers and coffee-houses, who, by refusing to take in the particular paper, rendered the Defence Committee most valuable assistance. The struggle extended over a considerable period, and was carried on by the Society in the most vigorous manner, the "minutes" of the Committee clearly showing that, had it not been for the energy displayed, other offices would have adopted the "new system" against the introduction of which the members were fighting. Addresses were distributed broadcast throughout the country, and posted in public houses and coffee shops in the metropolis, and at one time members of the "rat" ship were engaged to go round and collect the bills, stating that they were authorised to do so by the Defence Committee, as the employers had given way. Although a heavy expenditure had to be met, the members eventually had the satisfaction of attaining the desired result, the employer being badly beaten in his attempts to introduce a system of working at variance with the established customs of the trade.

The following year witnessed the long-delayed but much-desired amalgamation of the two societies, the Annual Report for 1854 announcing that in the preceding March the Old Daily News Society had joined the

London Society of Compositors—for which the circumstances referred to above were mainly responsible. The membership of the Society was thus increased to over 2,600 paying members, the subscription showing an increase in comparison with the preceding year of over £354.

Mention is also made of the National Typographical Emigration Society, which was brought into existence in the provinces in the early part of the year, and expired before its close, the sum of £110 being all that was contributed, its failure being attributed by the Committee to the fact that "the passage money was given, instead of being lent." At this period the Emigration Aid Committee was still carrying on its work, a "Public Drawing for Advances" taking place at the "Falcon" Tavern in June- the loans being fixed at sums of £15 and £30, the Committee pointing out that as many successful candidates had not availed themselves of the loan, and "by their thoughtless conduct" had deprived others of the advantage, it was intended to impose a fine of 10s. and 20s. respectively upon members not emigrating within the time specified by rule. The half-yearly report for 1853 showed that the fund had received £250 from the Trade Society (as a loan), and £34 0s. 3d. as the result of a benefit at Sadler's Wells Theatre; the sum of £231 having been advanced to emigrants; the expenditure including an item of 1s. 10d. "postage of letter from Melbourne."

Appended to this Report was the following:—
"The Committee having ascertained, upon undoubted authority, that the Society would be responsible for the

support of the wives or families of any members emigrating without them, beg to announce that under no circumstances whatever will advances be granted to married men about to emigrate without either their wives or families."

Beyond a grant of £200 to the Preston Operatives (supplemented later by a grant of £120), and £50 to the Belfast Society, there is little to notice until March of 1854, when, "in pursuance of a resolution of the late General Meeting," the Committee inform the trade that "the office of Secretary has become vacant by the resignation of Mr. Boyett." For the vacant position there were three candidates, the ballot resulting in the return of Mr. W. Cox (853 votes), who took office on the 3rd of April. At the preceding Delegate Meeting a resolution was agreed to "deeply regretting that the Society is about to lose the able counsel as well as the valuable and indefatigable exertions of Mr. Boyett, Secretary," and recommending the Committee "to take into consideration the means whereby the trade may best mark its esteem not only for his official services, but its respect for his private worth."

In 1854, an exceedingly interesting report was presented by a Select Committee which had been appointed by the Committee of the Society "to inquire into the origin of the Closing of Messrs. Spottiswoode's Houses," such report (which the delegates decided should be printed and circulated throughout the trade) being intended "for the information of the younger members of the trade, and those unacquainted with the merits of the dispute." It contained extracts from, and remarks upon, the evidence taken before the Select Committee of the House of Lords on Parliamentary Printing (June, 1854), with a "Sketch of the Nature of the Agreement to which the Contract Printer for Government has to subscribe."

To relieve the unemployed members, a sum of £200 was granted by the delegates, to be distributed at the rate of 10s. per week to members of the Provident Fund who had drawn the full allowance, and to members not belonging to the Fund who had paid a full year's subscription to the Society. In April of 1855, the delegates decided to form a Library, and appointed a "House Committee" from the members assembled to expend the sums voted for such purpose.

In the same month a communication was addressed to the members from the Provincial Typographical Association, signed by Wm. Dronfield (President), and Josephus Speak (Secretary), embodying certain resolutions passed at a Special Meeting held in Sheffield, to consider the propriety of sending "missionaries" throughout the provinces, "for the purpose of rousing the profession to the necessity of making more efficient provision for protecting our labour, and for limiting the number of apprentices in localities where no restriction now exists." The meeting especially urged their metropolitan brethren to enter into the movement and to appoint two delegates.

In June, the business of the Society was transferred from the "Falcon" Tavern, to No. 3, Racquet Court, Fleet Street, a special circular being sent out to the employers and overseers, directing attention to the arrangements which had been made "to render nugatory, as far as possible, the inconvenience sometimes occasioned to employers by too frequent inquiries after work by the unemployed," and "to relieve the workman from the necessity of perambulating from office to office in search of employment." A Reading Room was set apart for the use of members, and liberally supplied with newspapers and magazines, both metropolitan and provincial.

About this time the demands upon the Provident Fund were greatly in excess of the receipts, with the result that in September a Special Delegate Meeting was held, upon the requisition of 115 members, "to consider the present state of distress, and the best means of alleviating it," at which it was resolved to advance the sum of £150.

The granting of money to a fund from which the majority of the trade was not entitled to receive benefit gave rise to dissatisfaction, which found expression in a proposal submitted to the delegates in April, that in order that all members might be placed upon the same footing, " paying equal subscriptions, and entitled to equal benefits, it is advisable that the distinction between Provident and non-Provident members be now discontinued, and that the Provident be consolidated in the trade fund."

During the year the question of adopting Rules for the guidance of an Arbitration Committee had been considered on two occasions, and eventually resulted in the formation of a Committee, consisting of three employers and three journeymen, presided over by a barrister as chairman, appointed annually.

The Arbitration Rules came into force on the 1st of January, 1856, and at the July meeting the delegates were called upon to nominate twelve offices, from each of which should be forwarded the name of a person willing and qualified from acquaintance with the Scale and customs of the trade, to act as Arbitrator; the Trade Committee to be empowered to select from such list " Arbitrators in the three cases which have been, by a vote of the two Committees of Masters and Journeymen, referred to Arbitration." This Committee met August 5th, 1856, at Freemasons' Tavern, the question in dispute being the right of the compositor to the standing fat in chase of two volumes of "The Memoirs and Letters of Sydney Smith." Messrs. Harrison, Kinder, and Wyman, with Mr. J. A. D. Cox (Hon. Sec.) represented the employers; Messrs. Craig, Henley, and Knott, with Mr. W. Cox (Secretary) the journeymen. The first question was unanimously decided in favour of the compositors; the second against them, upon the casting vote of the Chairman (Mr. G. Sweet, of the Inner Temple), costs being divided.

On the 25th November, the Trade Committee found it necessary to draw the attention of their members to a Circular which had been issued by the Employers' Committee to the Master Printers of London, regarding the decision given in the case of standing advertisements, the Committee stating that no alteration had been made in the manner of charging such matter, and that the statement to the contrary in the Circular referred to was not in agreement with the generally-accepted reading of the Scale.

In the preceding year a Joint Committee had been appointed "to take evidence and devise means for the future protection of the News Trade," and in May, 1856, a lengthy and comprehensive report was presented by this "Amalgamated Committee," which embodied in it the rules and regulations the majority of which are in operation at the present time. A report of an equally lengthy nature was also drawn up by the minority, quite as exhaustive in its scope and recommendations as that presented by their colleagues, the point at issue, and upon which the members were acutely divided, being that of piece versus 'stab composition for full hands—three houses having been closed in opposition to the introduction of 'stab work.

A Special Delegate Meeting was convened for January 7th, 1857, to consider a proposition submitted from the Employers' Committee that a conference should be held "to settle the price that should be paid for cases in Chancery and the answers thereto, and of such other work connected with the Law Courts as is now, or may hereafter be ordered to be printed, which is at present written." The meeting, however, had to be postponed in consequence of the decease of Mr. Cox, the Secretary, and on the 14th of January a circular was issued inviting nominations for the vacant position. A Special General Meeting was fixed for Saturday evening, the 31st January, at the National Hall, Holborn, but three days prior an urgent circular was distributed notifying that, "in consequence of the Gallery of the National Hall having been, by the constituted authorities, declared unsafe," the meeting would take place in the Theatre of the Mechanics' Institution. The business included a proposal re the appointment of an Assistant Secretary, whose duties should combine those of Librarian and Housekeeper.

There were three candidates for the Secretaryship, the ballot resulting in the appointment of Mr. W. Beckett (of Clay's), the voting paper notifying that as the trade had decided to appoint a permanent Assistant Secretary, nominations for the post would be received at the next quarterly meeting. On the 4th of March, the newly-appointed Secretary issued a circular convening a Special Delegate Meeting for the 11th, "to take into consideration certain resolutions impugning the recent decision of the Trade Committee with respect to the election of the Secretary." At this meeting the decision referred to was annulled, it being agreed to proceed to a new election, and on the 18th of March it was announced that Ballot Papers would be ready on the 26th, and issued only to members less than 13 weeks in arrear. On this occasion there were two candidates, Mr. Beckett receiving 1,072 votes, and Mr. A. J. S. Headland (of Savill and Edwards) 982 votes.

Application was made to the members at the April meeting for the use of a room in which on alternate Monday evenings the business of a Permanent Sick Fund Union (then in course of formation) might be transacted, the object of the Union being to abolish the "petition and raffle system." About this time members were being urged to make the subscription of 2d. per week to the Provident Fund compulsory upon all members; and to discontinue the appointment of a distinct

Committee to manage the Emigration Aid Society, a meeting being held in July to consider the Trade Committee's proposal to wind up the affairs of the latter Society.

Serious disputes arose during the year 1857, mainly in connection with the charges for Chancery and Appeal Cases, affecting several large offices, and in October the provincial typographical societies were warned by circular not to permit their members to accept engagements in London pending the settlement of the "serious matters" then engaging the attention of the London Society, which early in the following year were settled at a Conference with the employers, whereby the office of Messrs. Woodfall and Kinder was re-opened to the members, that of Messrs. Spottiswoode and Co. remaining closed.

The question of standing advertisements in wrappers and advertising sheets had also continued to create friction, and was eventually settled by an action in the Court of Exchequer, the judgment of Mr. Baron Watson and Mr. Baron Channell, given on February 25th, 1858, upholding the claim made on behalf of the Society.

The Quarterly Meeting in March was asked to agree that "in consequence of the increase in the business of the establishment at 3, Racquet Court, both as a Trade Society and a Literary Institution, it is desirable that the Society should occupy the whole of the premises, and that the Trade Committee should give the Bookbinders notice to quit." A deputation attended from the Machine Managers' Society, requesting that their unemployed members might be permitted to use the Society House, the application being granted.

This meeting is also noticeable from the fact that the members decided to subscribe the sum of fourteen guineas to certain of the Metropolitan Medical Charities, thus initiating a grant which has been uninterruptedly maintained, and has steadily increased in amount year by year. In the balance sheet the sum of £10 is set out as a loan to the Dublin House Painters, a note explaining that the Dublin Society had repudiated the liability, "denying the authority of the parties who had contracted this and other loans;" also a donation of £5 to the library, "by the Chancellor of the Exchequer," and 5s. for the "use of room for raffles."

At the November Meeting, resolutions were passed protesting against the continuance of the Paper Duty, and deciding to petition Parliament for its repeal.

Unusual interest appears to have been manifested in the proceedings of the Annual Meeting, held on February 16th, 1859, as within a few days the members were notified that, "in consequence of the vote of the late General Meeting," the office of Secretary was vacant. The adjourned Annual Meeting was held on the 16th of March, the only business transacted being the re-election of the Assistant Secretary, and the consideration of a report and financial statement presented by two Auditors (Messrs. R. Lee and W. White) appointed by the Trade Committee, as distinct from the statement prepared by their late Secretary, and in which certain recommendations were embodied with a view to initiating a better method of keeping the Society's accounts, which were referred by the members to a "Committee of Inquiry," who reported to a Special General Meeting held in the month of June. Meanwhile, the election for the Secretaryship had taken place, resulting in the re-election of Mr. Beckett, Mr. H. Self being the only other candidate.

In consequence of a decision given by Mr. Russell Gurney (Recorder of the City of London), the Trade Committee, in November, advised the members that as such decision was entirely opposed to the spirit and, in their opinion, to the letter of the Scale, they must decline "undertaking on the piece the composition of books of reference, lists of voters, or any similar work, unless paid for as table." The matter was considered at a Special Delegate Meeting, held in January, 1860, when it was resolved to close the office in which the disputed question had arisen, and to warn society men against accepting work there "until further notice."

The working hours came under consideration at the Annual Meeting held in 1860, when it was proposed " that the day's work should commence at eight o'clock in the morning and end at eight in the evening, and that all extra time beyond that period be paid for at the rate of 3*d*. per hour extra," the members, however, rejecting it. It was agreed that the delegates should not have power to grant a larger sum than £30 "without a ballot of the members;" a Special Committee being appointed to enquire into the working of the Provident Fund. The membership was then 2,550, "none of whom exceeded thirteen weeks' arrears."

Early in 1860 a scheme of Superannuation was drawn up by "a sincere friend and member" of the Society, and discussed at a meeting held at the "Welsh Harp," Bouverie Street, when it was decided to print and circulate the scheme to the trade, an adjourned meeting taking place on the 3rd of April to further discuss the matter. In addition to the Superannuation benefit (which could be claimed twelve months after the fund was established), it was proposed to create a Funeral benefit, and to place the Provident Fund under the control of the Trade Committee—the latter suggestion being adopted at a Special General Meeting held in the Great Hall of the Whittington Club, Arundel Street, Strand, in September, when the "Rules of the Provident Fund Department" were finally agreed upon, after considerable opposition had been shown towards the introduction of benefits, as tending to "a complete and universal upsetting of the principles of the Society—our actions being directed to the protection of our labour—in plainer words, securing the means by which we live."

Towards the end of the year, the Committee issued a recommendation that "Members holding regular situations, and being in full work, should not take work in other offices after eight o'clock at night, or on Sundays."

Although the work of the Society continued to be transacted at Racquet Court until 1893, it is interesting to note that at the Thirteenth Annual Meeting, held in 1861, a proposition was submitted from a chapel to the effect that "as the lease of the premises held by the Society at Racquet Court will expire in a few months — this meeting, deeming such premises to be ineligible for the fully carrying out of the advantages which the trade might possess, even with the present expenditure — hereby requests the Executive to obtain information as to the attainment of a more suitable building, as well as probable expenses, locality, etc.," and to report to a Special General Meeting, which was duly convened for the purpose on the 16th of June; a deputation being also appointed from this meeting to attend a Meeting of Delegates of the Typographical Societies of the United Kingdom, held at Manchester on July 22nd and four following days, Messrs. W. Beckett and H. Self (Book), and W. M. Dean (News) being the selected delegates.

In December a Ballot Paper was issued with regard to the building or leasing new premises for a Society House, the Committee referring to the thin attendance (less than 100) at both special meetings, and reporting against the change, on the grounds that the locality was central, the rental lower than that of any other suitable building in the neighbourhood, and the funds being impaired through giving between £800 and £900 to the unemployed members, in addition to the Provident Fund relief, the result being that the lease of the old premises was renewed, 1,437 papers being returned, showing 1,433 in favour of renewing the lease, 1,430 being in favour of an alternative proposal that the future balances of receipts over expenditure should be reserved towards buying or building new premises.

On the 21st, the members were notified that a dispute existed in the office of Messrs. Woodfall and Kinder, involving a serious infraction of the Trade Scale and Customs, a Special Meeting being held on the 31st to consider the course of action to be adopted.

As an outcome of the meeting held in Manchester, a proposal was submitted to a ballot of the trade in

March of 1862, regarding the Tramping System—the object being to adopt a general relief payment of 1d. per mile, which was rejected by 1,078 to 514. By the same ballot the members (by 815 to 757) decided to advance the sum of £400 to the Paris Typographical Society.

At the February (1863) meeting a further attempt was made to incorporate the Provident Fund with the Trade Society, a Special Committee being appointed "to investigate and consider the best means to obviate Trade Grants to the Unemployed." Their report was submitted to the August Delegate Meeting, and a ballot taken, when it was decided by 1,373 votes to 349 to amalgamate the Trade and Provident Funds, the scheme coming into operation in October, and the maximum subscription being increased from 4d. to 6d. per week.

In July, continued ill-health caused Mr. Beckett to resign the Secretaryship, the Committee inviting the members assembled at the Annual Meeting in 1864 to give consideration to "the late Secretary's application for further pecuniary assistance in his present trying position," who had had to resign the duties of his office through "sheer exhaustion." The trade generously decided that Mr. Beckett should continue to receive two-thirds of his salary.

For the vacant position, the names of two candidates were submitted to the ballot—Messrs. H. Self and W. Hinds, the former being declared elected on the 6th of April. Three months later a report was presented by a Special Committee which had been appointed " for the purpose of considering the best means of reconstructing the Executive," in which it was proposed that the Trade Committee should be appointed at the Annual Meeting (the objection to the chapel-electing system being that the smaller offices were almost entirely excluded), and that a Chairman should likewise be elected annually.

These proposals were placed upon the Business Paper of the Seventeenth Annual Meeting, held in February, 1865, and referred to a Special Delegate Meeting held during the following month, and rejected.

In December of 1865 a Special Committee (presided over by Mr. C. Henley) was appointed to draw up a Memorial to the employers, requesting an advance of $\frac{1}{2}d$. per thousand, and a reduction of the working hours to sixty per week. This Memorial was presented to the employers in the following January, and in May a Conference was held, the results being referred to the members at a General Meeting convened in August, and declined. In September, it was decided by ballot to double the subscription for three months; and, later, a proposal was received from the employers that the Conference should be re-opened. This the members, at a General Meeting held in Exeter Hall on October 23rd, declined to accede to, and the Committee intimated that, unless the terms of the Memorial were granted, instructions would be given that it should become operative on and after the second Monday in November. Further negotiations took place, and fresh proposals submitted on the part of the employers, which were accepted as the basis of a settlement, arrived at on the 21st of November, whereby an advance of $\frac{1}{2}d$. per thousand on all descriptions of work (excepting newspapers) was gained, the 'stab wage being raised to 36s., and the working hours reduced to sixty per week. Unfortunately, the agreement thus arrived at was not accepted by all the employers, with the result that about half-a-dozen offices were closed to the Society.

During the following year a Special Committee had under consideration "the practicability of a scheme for the payment of sums of money ranging from £5 to £12 to representatives of deceased members," and in February, 1868, the delegates were invited to agree "That the time had arrived when a moderate superannuation allowance should be made to members who, from age or infirmity, ought not to be sent to a call." With respect to the first question, a ballot was taken in April, when it was agreed, by 916 votes to 390, that a Death Allowance should be added to the Society's benefits, to come into operation on the 5th of October, the maximum subscription being raised to 7d. per week.

An important report was presented during the same year by a Committee appointed by the Newsmen (with two representatives from the Book Department) to "Revise the Trade Rules, examine into the system of working in each office, and frame a report upon the evidence that may come before them."

Owing to the death of Mr. J. Shand in 1869, the Assistant-Secretaryship became vacant, the position being filled by the election of Mr. J. Borer, out of eight candidates nominated.

In August the members were called upon to consider a report of a Special Committee " upon the constitution and working of the amalgamated trades, the central offices of which are in London, with a view (if practicable and advisable) to a thorough reorganisation of the London Society of Compositors on the basis of amalgamation." The proposed scheme comprised provident, sick, superannuation, emigration, and funeral benefits.

Serious difficulties arose during the early part of 1870, the Trade Committee being called upon to deal with an employer who, although one of the signatories to the Scale agreed upon in 1866, declined to be further bound by certain of its essential provisions. As there appeared to be danger of a combined effort being made to reduce wages (three houses being involved in the dispute), steps were immediately taken to protect the trade, the subscriptions being doubled for a period of six weeks, warning circulars being issued to provincial societies, and a Special General Meeting convened at the Cannon Street Hotel, at which resolutions of a drastic character were submitted and approved. As a consequence, the dispute did not (as was at one time feared) become general, although at the same time proving a heavy drain upon the Society's funds, which formed the subject of discussion at a Special Meeting, held at the Sussex Hotel in December, when a report was submitted on "the present prospects of the Society, with suggestions for strengthening its position, and extending the means for alleviating the condition of its unemployed members."

In January, 1871, several propositions were submitted to a ballot, with the result that members drawing full provident benefit for three years in succession were placed upon half-pay, with a probationary period of two years for new members (other than apprentices);

removal and emigration allowances were established, and a scheme of amalgamation with the Machine Managers' and Pressmen's Societies agreed upon. A sliding scale of subscriptions (3*d*. to 9*d*.) was rejected in favour of a uniform contribution of 7*d*. per week.

PRINTERS' ART UNION ASSOCIATION.

For many years the inadequate accommodation at the Racquet Court premises had been a constant source of regret, and on the 29th of September, 1871, a meeting was convened with the laudable object of devising means whereby more commodious premises might be secured. The result was the formation of the "Printers' Art Union Association," the rules of which contemplated " the provision of means for the erection of a building for the use of the members of the London Society of Compositors, and others to whom the privilege may be extended, and that the building shall consist of a hall, library, and reading rooms, with the necessary offices attached thereto." A Committee of twelve was appointed (with power to add to their number) from the members of the Society ; the price of the subscription tickets being fixed at 1*s*. each, and the value of the prizes (consisting of articles within the range of literature and art) at from £1 to £5.

The first Report, presented on August 3rd, 1872, referred to the "meagreness of the response" made by the members to the "several appeals" issued by the Association Committee, two special meetings having likewise failed to stimulate interest in the matter. A circular appeal was drawn up and issued "to the whole of the Members of both Houses of Parliament and other eminent persons," the 1,200 copies thus distributed resulting in the receipt of one donation of £25. The first balance sheet showed that a profit of £108 11s. had been secured towards the realisation of the object in view.

In the following year, a deputation waited upon the kindred trades in the metropolis, with the desire of obtaining their assistance in making the movement a success, which from this period appears to have made rapid progress, the sixth annual drawing, which took place at the Cannon Street Hotel on the 24th of March, 1877, being attended by about 700 persons, the balance sheet showing that a sum of about £3,700 had been raised, of which £360 had been paid as a deposit on signing a contract for " 3,600 superficial feet of freehold land in Eagle Street, Red Lion Street, Holborn, the intended site for the building—the object of the Association," a further sum of £3,240 (balance of purchase money) having to be paid on the 1st of September. Over 1,200 persons attended the following annual drawing, the first prize being of the value of £60, the second of £50, and the remainder ranging from £30 to 10s. 6d., the prizes numbering 700.

Although the results of the various drawings gave every indication of enabling the Committee to bring their labours to a successful termination, the site chosen for the proposed Society House proved thoroughly unsuitable, difficulties arising on every hand—the question of "ancient lights" threatening to lead to legal complications. The circumstances under which the property had been purchased formed the subject of lengthy and continuous correspondence, noticeable for a denial of responsibility on the part of those whose legal assistance had been relied upon throughout the negotiations for its purchase; and the Committee eventually reported to the members of the Association "that to attempt to utilise the land in Eagle Street for the purpose originally intended would be to surround you with difficulties and liabilities from which it would be impossible to release you without involving such sacrifices as the result would not justify," and advised that the land should be sold "for what it will fetch."

At the Thirty-second Annual General Meeting of the Society, held on March the 3rd, 1880, a resolution was passed by an overwhelming majority, which referred to the ill-feeling existing in the trade regarding the "unsatisfactory working of the Printers' National Art Union," and called upon the paid officers of the Society "to cease connection" with the Association. In agreement with this resolution, the Working Committee of the Art Union decided that the next prize drawing should be the final one, and that the books of the Association should be examined, and a report presented to the Trade Committee.

Finally, in June of 1886, a statement was circulated showing the manner in which the affair had been wound up. The freehold land had been sold for £2,100, and the sum of £1,375 (advanced towards its purchase) repaid to the Society, leaving a balance of £775, which was distributed *pro rata*, the London Society of Compositors (6,500 members) receiving £650, the Machine Managers' Association (1,000 members) £100, and the Amalgamated Society of Pressmen (250 members) £25.

NINE HOURS MOVEMENT.

Towards the close of the year 1871 a Circular was addressed to chapels with regard to the propriety and expediency of reducing the working hours to fifty-four per week, in order that the views of the general body of members might be elicited upon the subject. In January of 1872 a Memorial was presented to the employers through the various chapels (the Employers' Association having ceased to exist). As the result of a meeting held at the Freemasons' Tavern (at which the employers appointed a Committee to consider the Memorial), counter-proposals were presented to those put forward on behalf of the members, and considered and unanimously adopted at a meeting held at Exeter Hall on March the 6th, whereby (in addition to the reduction of hours) an advance of ½d. per thousand was secured on all descriptions of composition (other than news and parliamentary work), overtime commencing after seven o'clock (two o'clock on Saturdays).

After this successful effort, matters proceeded smoothly until 1874, when the question of an advance in prices (with payment for slating and 3d. per hour extra for Sunday work) engaged the attention of the daily and weekly paper hands. After several meetings had been held, the various questions were submitted to a ballot, the rise per thousand and the "slating" proposals being endorsed by large majorities, the extra for Sunday work on daily papers finding very few supporters. In

June a memorial was forwarded to the Proprietors and Printers of the Weekly Papers, as well as to the Proprietors of the London Daily Papers. The former appointed a Committee to meet the men's representatives, and eventually modified proposals were submitted and accepted, the working hours being fixed at fifty-four, piece hands to receive 3*d.* per hour after sixty hours had been worked, and the Scale in other respects being materially improved.

Nothing of particular note occupied attention until 1876, when, at the May meeting (the first held in the Memorial Hall), a proposition was placed upon the Business Paper, at the request of an evening paper chapel, suggesting the appointment of a Special Committee to consider the desirability of adding superannuation to the benefits of the Society. This course was adopted, the consideration of this important subject being entrusted to nine members, who, in the following September, presented a report bearing evidence that the most careful and minute investigations had been made into the various points involved in the launching of a successful and satisfactory scheme of superannuation benefits. Two special meetings were devoted to its discussion, and in October three propositions were submitted to a Ballot—the first fixing the benefit for partially-incapacitated members of twenty years' standing at 4*s.* per week, twenty-five years' membership, 5*s.* per week; the second dealing with totally-incapacitated members, whose allowances were to be—after fifteen years' membership, 4*s.*; twenty years', 5*s.*; and thirty years', 10*s.* per week; the third, fixing their subscriptions at 1*d.* per week. In the printed report for February, 1877, appears the names of the first eight members placed upon the Superannuation Fund, the youngest aged sixty-two, and the oldest eighty, each of whom (with one exception) were receiving 5*s.* per week.

Early in 1877, a Special Committee reported upon the important question of Apprenticeship, this being the fifth Committee which had been appointed to inquire into the same subject during a period of forty years. This report was likewise of a particularly exhaustive character, and contained a recommendation that, in order to check the "turnover" system, the Society should recognise and encourage a five-years' term of apprenticeship; at the same time pointing out that, in adopting remedial measures, the utmost consideration and forethought was necessary, in order that the support and goodwill of fair employers might be retained in the attempt to exercise a gradual influence upon those employers who were indifferent to the interests of the trade as a whole.

In the same year, the question of calling upon establishment hands to write a "line" bill was raised, the endeavour of the Executive to stop the system having been met by a suggestion on the part of one large firm that the matter should be referred to arbitration —a suggestion which eventually was accepted by the Society. Mr. T. Hughes, Q.C., was appointed Arbitrator, his award (given on the 3rd of July, 1877) declaring "that no reasonable or sufficient grounds had been shown for altering, against the wishes of the firm in whose house the question had arisen, the existing practice of 'stab hands marking the lines on their wages bills."

Towards the end of 1877, members were invited to consider the propriety of appointing an additional permanent officer, and at the Delegate Meeting in February, 1878, rules were presented defining the duties which should devolve upon the Financial Secretary. At this meeting the annual appointment of a Chairman was considered; also the propriety of registering the Society under the Trade Union Act of 1871, as well as the appointment of a Building Committee to carry out the details involved in the erection of suitable premises on the Society's freehold land in Eagle Street, Holborn, the Machine Managers' and Pressmen's Unions being invited to send delegates to co-operate with the Society's representatives. In May, Mr. C. J. Drummond was elected to the position of Assistant Secretary; Mr. T. J. Thompson being appointed Chairman.

In November of 1878, the propriety of increasing the relief to all London compositors "taking the road" from ½d. to 1d. per mile was discussed, also the raising of the unemployed allowance from 10s. to 12s., and increasing the number of weeks from thirteen to sixteen, the latter proposal being agreed to. With regard to the former proposal, some correspondence passed with the Executive Council of the Typographical Association, who were averse to the increased payment on the ground that "it would naturally tend to swamp the districts covered by the Association with the unemployed of the London Society during the oft-recurring periods of stagnation in the London trade, and would in other ways be opposed to the interests of the members of the Typographical Association," the Council therefore declining to consider any conditions by which such a change could be effected.

The business occupying the attention of the delegates in November of 1879 included a proposal that an Association should be formed, to be called "The Federation of Organised Trade Societies," having for its object "the establishment of a fund for the maintenance of the present Nine Hours System."

In March of 1880, the weekly subscription was raised to 8*d*. for a period of twelve months; and a vacancy arising through the resignation of Mr. Thompson, Mr. Richard Lee was elected to the position of Chairman. In August, a Special Committee was appointed to inquire into the financial condition of the Society, their report being submitted in the early part of the following year. After referring to the large increase in the Society's benefits, whereas formerly it existed solely for the purpose of protecting the trade from the arbitrary encroachments of employers, the Committee recommended that investments to the extent of £5,000 should be made upon freehold and leasehold properties, in preference to Consols; that the maximum Superannuation payment should be lowered from 10*s*. to 6*s*., and the entitling membership increased to thirty-five years, and that the fund should be separated from the Society, *i.e.*, worked by a separate Committee, with a view to its being made self-supporting; and that the weekly subscription should be permanently increased to 8*d*.; advising also that the system of travelling relief should be abolished, and that the probationary period of persons entering at the age of thirty should be two years, with a further twelve months' probation for every additional five years, before a member could be entitled to claim Provident benefit. It was also recommended that the minimum capital of the Society should be fixed at £2, with power to levy if at any time necessary. Fourteen questions were submitted to the ballot, the whole of them being endorsed by very large majorities, the vote upon the proposed reduction of the superannuation benefit showing the narrowest majority.

At the Annual Meeting of 1881, two names were placed in nomination for the position of Librarian and Housekeeper, the subsequent ballot resulting in the return of Mr. A. G. Cook. Up to this period, all investments had been made and held in the names of stockholders, who eventually numbered over seventy. At a Special General Meeting, held in August, it was decided that in future the property and funds belonging to the Society should be vested in the names of four Trustees, the gentlemen honoured with the confidence of the members being Messrs. J. Melhuish, J. R. Meyer, C. J. Radley, and R. J. Townsend. In the same year a Memorial was addressed to the Lords of the Treasury, relating to the Contracts for Printing Parliamentary Papers.

The lengthened illness of Mr. Self was the subject of consideration at the November Quarterly Meeting, when the Committee, regretting that they saw no immediate prospect of that gentleman resuming his duties as Secretary, and feeling also that his present state of health is almost or entirely due to the strenuous exertions he has at all times put forth in the interests of the Society, "recommended that he should be granted a retiring allowance of 30s. per week for life." The discussion resulted in the modified proposal of £50 per annum being submitted to the ballot, and agreed to by an overwhelming majority. At a later period, Mr. Self was the recipient of a testimonial and address, presented to him by the members "as a slight acknowledgment of the valuable services rendered by him as Secretary, during a period of seventeen years, during which time he had by the faithful discharge of his duties, his upright conduct, strict impartiality and great ability, deservedly obtained the respect and esteem of all with whom he had been in any way officially connected, whose sincere thanks are hereby tendered to him upon his retirement from office."

For the vacancy thus created in the Secretaryship, two candidates were nominated at the Special General Meeting held on the 16th of November, and afterwards submitted to a ballot, the election resulting in favour of Mr. C. J. Drummond (who previously had resigned the Assistant-Secretaryship), the unsuccessful candidate being Mr. W. A Coote. For the latter position, four names were placed before the trade, the successful candidate being Mr. C. Morley.

A year later, it became necessary to again ballot the members in connection with the Assistant-Secretaryship, the election resulting in the return of Mr. G. W. Banks.

At the Annual Meeting held in March, 1883, the Committee invited the members to adopt a Trade Emblem, to be supplied as a certificate of membership, a desire for which had been expressed by a large number of members. At the same meeting, reference was made to the death of Mr. J. C. Yeoman, who had for a number of years occupied the honourable position of Treasurer to the Society; the vacant position being filled a few weeks later by the election of Mr. J. Woozley.

The subject of Arbitration engaged the attention of a Special General Meeting on the 3rd of April, when a proposition was discussed that a Board should be established in connection with the letterpress branch of printing, to which all trade disputes, and all matters of disagreement between employer and employed could be submitted, the decisions of such Board (consisting of thirteen members, six employers, six journeymen, and a chairman) to be binding on both parties.

A movement of some importance sprang from a proposal submitted by the Committee to the Delegate Meeting in November, 1883, dealing with the constitution of the Committee, which resulted in the appointment of a Special Committee empowered to "consider the best means of propounding a scheme for the reconstitution of the Executive." The direction in which this Committee desired the members to act is shown in the business placed before the newsmen at their Annual Meeting in February, 1884, which included the consideration of an interim report from the Special Committee, in which the "desirability was expressed that in future the Society should be governed by one Executive, elected by the members generally, and under one code of Rules; applicable equally to all members, irrespective of the particular branch of the business in which they may from time to time be employed." The members of the News Branch passed a resolution expressing extreme disapproval of the suggestion for the absorption of their members with the general body, as being likely to cause dissension, and tending to separate the two bodies, "a result that would be much to be regretted."

It was not, however, until May of 1884, that the report of the Committee came before the general trade for consideration. It proposed that an Executive Council of nine members should be elected annually by ballot, and that one of the number should be elected as President, to preside over the meetings of the Council, and at all General and Delegate Meetings. Carefully drawn rules were framed to govern the method of nomination, election, etc., the majority of which have since been embodied in the rules; and certain fines were suggested—(1) 2s. 6d. if a member of the Council was proved to have disclosed Executive business before a decision had been arrived at, and for a second offence, removal from the Board and disqualification from again holding a seat for a period of twelve months; (2) one guinea, with disqualification for two years, if a candidate for office canvassed for votes outside his own particular chapel, or was detected in offering a bribe with a view to obtaining any office.

A ballot was taken in July upon the propriety of the members taking part in an important Demonstration of the Trades in connection with the Great Reform Demonstration in Hyde Park, a very narrow majority, upon a small vote, deciding in favour of "demonstrating."

At the Annual Meeting in 1885, the Trade Committee advised that the Society should become affiliated with the London Trades' Council, a deputation from the executive of that body attending the meeting for the purpose of addressing the members, who eventually decided in favour of affiliation. At the same meeting an application was considered from the Librarian and Housekeeper, who desired to remove from the Society House, " and to take up his residence elsewhere, subject to the appointment of a Caretaker in whom the Committee may feel sufficient confidence."

It was agreed that the Society House and Reading Room should be closed at nine (instead of ten) o'clock, from Monday to Friday, and on Saturdays at three o'clock (previously four).

Towards the end of 1885 a serious dispute arose, involving the convening of a special meeting to consider the steps rendered necessary in the interests of the trade generally. During this struggle an attempt was made to bring about a Federation of the Printing and Paper Trades, on the lines laid down in 1870, when it was hoped, by means of an Amalgamated Society of Printers, "to gather together, in one vast organisation, the whole of the members of the three branches of the business, not in London only, but throughout the United Kingdom," which at the time was rejected by the trade. With regard to the revived scheme, several meetings were held, and rules drafted, the Federation comprising sixteen societies, having a membership of 11,196.

From time to time the Rules of the Society underwent alteration, and among the changes or additions agreed upon at the Delegate Meeting in February, 1886, were—a rule prohibiting a member holding a full-frame from working for any other employer; insisting upon members paying their subscriptions through the chapel in which they were working; and dealing with "members ratting" (a matter not then provided for by rule) by introducing a clause clearly defining the penalty incurred by members accepting work in an "unfair" office; also a rule setting forth the course to be pursued towards members suspected of defrauding the Society.

In the same year the Government appointed a Royal Commission to inquire into the Depression of Trade and Industry, Mr. Drummond, in conjunction with Mr. T. Birtwistle, being appointed upon it to represent the labour interest.

Upon the death of Mr. Richard Lee, in July, 1886, the Committee recommended the members to abolish the office of Chairman of the Society, and to revert to the custom existing prior to 1878, when the Committee elected their own Chairman. At the August Delegate Meeting, however, this suggestion met with little favour, and it was decided to proceed to the election of a Chairman, for which position seven members were nominated, the ballot resulting in the return of Mr. R. W. Minter. At this meeting the members were invited to appoint delegates to attend an International Trade Union Congress in Paris, organised by the French Labour Party.

Later in the year (October), a Typographical Conference was held in the Memorial Hall, at which several matters of importance were considered, namely, the necessity of reciprocity between the various Typographical Societies in the payment of out-of-work and sick benefits to travelling or invalided members; the effect of the use of stereotype in newspapers; the formation of a National Association; the jurisdiction of societies in dealing with the admission of unfair hands; the position of non-unionists, and how to secure their adhesion to the Union; the employment of machinemen only (who had served the customary apprenticeship) upon newspapers; also of women as compositors, etc., the Conference extending over three days.

For some years an acute division had prevailed between the Edinburgh compositors and the letterpress printers, resulting in 1873 in the formation by the latter body of a separate organisation. This question was also dealt with at the Conference, the Secretaries of the Typographical Association, the London Society of Compositors, and of the Machine Managers' and Pressmen's Societies, being appointed as Arbitrators, who met in Edinburgh in the following April, and in their Award, laid down the conditions under which the two societies should again be united.

Prior to 1887, correspondence had passed between the Society and the Controller of the Stationery Office, relative to the manner in which the printing work of the Government was being produced, most of the contracts having for years been practically monopolised by a house which declined to recognise the rules and customs of the London trade. The question had been vigorously followed up in the House of Commons by Mr. Henry Broadhurst, and in the Annual Report for 1887 the satisfactory statement was made that one of the large contracts had been taken from the non-society house by a recognised firm, employing none but members of the Society, and who had opened a very large office for the express purpose of carrying out the work required under the contract.

At the Annual Meeting for this year the question of the Half-pay Provident Allowance was discussed, the members deciding to expunge from the Rules the section dealing with that particular benefit ; but upon submitting the proposal to a ballot (a course to which strong exception appears to have been taken), the trade decided, by a small majority, to reverse the decision of the meeting. In the following March, however, the question was again submitted to a ballot, and it was decided by a majority of more than two to one, to abolish the half-pay system of Provident Relief.

Another matter giving rise to considerable discussion at this meeting had reference to the expenditure for printing during the year, which the report noted as having been unusually heavy, at the same time entering into the details of the quantity of work which the occurrences of the year had rendered unavoidable. The members, however, appointed a Special Committee to inquire into the matter, whose report (with a statement on behalf of the Executive) was presented to the trade in the following August, their conclusions being embodied in four proposals, with two of which the Executive were in complete agreement, and which (being approved by the members) have ever since been in operation—the main recommendation being the appointment of a Finance Committee, to be elected from the Trade Committee, a proposal brought forward at a later period that the members of the sub-committee should be appointed from the body of the trade, and not by the Committee, being rejected.

Four questions (submitted in agreement with a resolution passed at the Swansea Trade Union Congress) were referred to a ballot of the members in February, 1888, the results of which are not without interest, each of them being answered in the negative. For the first, "Are you in favour of an eight hours limit of the day's work—total forty-eight hours per week?" there voted 1,125, against 2,098; for the alternative proposal, "Are you in favour of a total cessation from work on Saturdays?" 319 voted in favour, 2,715 against; for "Are you in favour of Parliament enforcing an eight hours day by law, or enforcing a Saturday holiday by law?" 560 affirmative and 2,566 negative votes were recorded; and "In favour of obtaining either of these privileges by the free and united efforts of the organised trades of the kingdom?" 882 approved, and 2,146 disapproved.

Important amendments of rules were drafted by the Committee in the same year, and were referred to the delegates attending the adjourned August Meeting. By these proposals the accommodation hitherto provided at Racquet Court for the transaction of business of other societies was withdrawn, and, in addition to many alterations in the general rules, it was proposed that the Trade Committee should in future be elected half-yearly, and by ballot, instead of, as hitherto, the delegates electing by show of hands at the May and November meetings, three members to serve upon the Committee, at the same time appointing three chapels, each of which sent a representative. The principle of election by ballot was finally endorsed, and made annual instead of half-yearly; the attendance fee being also raised from 2s. to 3s. per sitting. With the same ballot paper, members were invited to state whether or not they were in favour of an eight-hour working day, 2,201 voting in favour and 1,411 against; the question "Are you in favour of its being obtained by Act of Parliament?" being answered in the affirmative by 1,578 members, and in the negative by 561.

At the November meeting, the Committee submitted a scheme whereby the Superannuation allowances could be increased, and the maximum payment again be fixed at 10s. per week, but the delegates decided to refer it back for re-consideration.

In the following year, the members of the Trade Committee were, for the first time, elected by ballot, an interesting feature of the contest being the fact that the names of seventy candidates were submitted to the trade—an evidence of the additional interest and enthusiasm which the adoption of a democratic system of election had imparted to a contest upon the results of which the future welfare of the Society to a large extent depended.

Successful efforts were being put forth at this period to induce public bodies to confine their work to employers recognised as "fair," and the results may best be realised when it is stated that a joint manifesto was addressed to the leading daily journal, signed by fourteen employers of non-union labour, to which a most spirited reply was made in a letter signed by three employers of union labour, defending the position which had been taken up by the Society upon this important matter.

A Conference was convened in 1889 to deal principally with the question of "slating" in daily paper offices, and also with the regulations governing evening paper work, delegates having previously been appointed from each newspaper office to inquire into the various subjects, and to report to the News Committee. The results of the inquiry were embodied in a Memorial to the employers, and although the discussions at the Conference failed to secure a recognition of payment for "slating" time, the conditions applying to evening paper work were much improved, the ordinary working hours being clearly defined, and overtime charges fixed for both evening and morning paper hands.

A further effort to increase the allowances to superannuated members was made in 1889, and, as the result of a ballot taken in November, the maximum payment was raised to 8s. per week. At the same time it was agreed, also upon the recommendation of the Trade Committee, to appoint an additional officer, rendered necessary by the growth of the Society's membership. The names of eight candidates were submitted to the vote, which resulted in the return of Mr. H. G. Weir. In consequence, however, of an indiscreet speech delivered by the member at an open-air demonstration, the Committee did not deem it advisable to permit the newly-elected officer to enter upon his duties, recommending that the office should remain vacant until the

Annual Meeting, or until after the incident had been considered by the members attending the next Quarterly Meeting.

Meanwhile, Mr. Cook had resigned the position of Librarian, and a sub-committee having carefully inquired into the duties of the office, recommended that two Assistants should be appointed, one of whom should take charge of the Library, and attend to petition fund business, and that the housekeeper should be appointed by and under the control of the Committee, instead of as hitherto holding the appointment through the Librarian. These suggestions were endorsed at a Special Delegate Meeting, and in March, 1890, Messrs. T. E. Peacock and W. H. Thorne (out of four candidates) were declared duly elected.

ADVANCE OF WAGES MOVEMENT, 1891.

The question of endeavouring to improve the conditions under which they were working had for some time engaged the attention of the Committee and the members, and at the Delegate Meeting held in February, 1890, it was unanimously resolved, upon the recommendation of the Trade Committee, to take a plebiscite on the propriety of approaching the employers with reference to an Advance of Wages. On the 11th of the month, Ballot Papers were issued, in which nine questions were submitted, all being answered in the affirmative—favouring a rise in the 'stab and piece rates, reducing systematic overtime by increasing the extra rates for such work, assimilating the book and weekly paper rates for overtime work, and reducing the maximum working hours, the co-operation of the Machine Managers' and Pressmen's Unions being invited in the effort to carry these proposals to a successful issue. As an evidence of the earnestness with which the members entered upon the Advance of Wages Movement, it was agreed that the subscriptions should be doubled for a period of thirteen weeks ; or for such further period as the Committee might deem necessary.

On the 24th of November a Memorial was addressed to the employers, setting forth the various provisions of the Scale which it was desired should be amended, and commending them to their favourable consideration, at the same time suggesting that the members were prepared to meet them " either individually or through the medium of a representative committee." The task of revising the Scale had been entrusted by the Trade Committee to a sub-committee of four of its members, with the Chairman and Secretary, assisted by four representative members, who were selected as possessing a special knowledge of the Scale and customs of the trade, and who, in presenting to the Committee a clear and concise report of their labours, claimed " that they had not attempted anything heroic," but had rather endeavoured to submit such amendments of the Scale as were likely to meet with the approval of the members, as well as with that of the employers, " for we are cognisant that no settlement of a permanent nature can be arrived at except with the consent of both parties."

The Memorial prepared on behalf of the members (the terms of which were clearly, comprehensively, and skilfully drawn) was received by the employers in a friendly manner, its tone and spirit materially assisting to convince them of the reasonableness of the claims submitted for their consideration. Correspondence ensued between the Society and the Printing and Allied Trades' Association, the latter body eventually appointing a Committee to meet a like number of representatives from the Society to discuss the terms of the Memorial, their contention that a Scale which had taken some months to revise could not be considered and become operative by the 1st of January being accepted as a reasonable one, the time consequently being extended to the 1st of March.

The Conference meeting was fixed for the 26th of January, 1891, at Stationers' Hall, and continued to sit, almost without interruption, until the 12th of February, and resulted in securing to the trade many substantial advantages to piece hands, with an all-round increase of 2s. per week to establishment hands, and solid increases in the rates for overtime work. The Agreement thus arrived at was submitted to a ballot of the members on the 17th of February, who, by a majority of 4,891 (the numbers being 6,187 against 1,296) gave their representatives full power to sign the Revised Scale, effect being given to this decision on the following day.

Considerable controversy arose after the Scale had been signed, which found expression at the Annual Meeting which was fixed to take place as usual at the Memorial Hall, the attendance being so great that it was decided to adjourn in order that a larger hall might be engaged. The adjourned meeting was held on Saturday afternoon, the 14th of March, at the Great Assembly Hall, Mile

End Road, the proceedings throughout being of the most turbulent and noisy character. The whole discussion centred upon an amendment "to strike out of the Annual Report all reference to the Advance of Wages," which was rejected in favour of a resolution calling upon the Executive to furnish an explanation of their action in the matter, and, in the event of such explanation being deemed unsatisfactory, to resign at once, this resolution being the outcome of a suggestion that the Executive had obtained a majority in the ballot for the signing of the Revised Scale "through the suppression of material facts connected therewith."

On the 24th of March, the Committee issued an explanatory statement, and asked the members to vote upon the question, "Are you satisfied with the Committee's explanation?" the answer being, "Yes," 4,389; "No," 1,645. At the adjourned meeting, held in the same hall on the 18th of April, the validity of this ballot was questioned on the ground that the vote had been taken at a time when the Society was "without a Secretary and other officials," their terms of office having expired in March, and "their names not having been submitted for re-election," which, it was contended, rendered the ballot null and void. The proceedings were, however, marked by comparative quietness, the members settling down to the transaction of the business for which the meeting had been convened.

Circumstances have since assuredly proved the wisdom of the members in accepting the settlement which their Executive had secured for them, after keen negotiations with the employers, and hostile opposition on the part of many of their constituents, and it is particularly gratifying to remember that the Advance of Wages Movement was brought to a successful conclusion without the loss of a single office.

Although at a later period some differences of opinion arose between the Society and the Masters' Association upon the interpretation to be placed upon the word "works" in Art. 27, as well as upon the application of certain of the overtime clauses in the Scale, they were eventually satisfactorily settled as the result of a further meeting, the decisions arrived at being embodied in a Minute signed on the 1st of September.

During the summer of 1891, owing to the efforts put forth by the Society, and with the cordial assistance of friends on the Council, the work of the London County Council, the contract for which had been secured by a notoriously "unfair" firm, was removed to a recognised house.

A Special Committee, which had been appointed at the Annual Meeting to inquire into and, if possible, simplify and improve the Call Book regulations, also reported in June, but their recommendations, which were intended to "popularise" the Call Book, by adopting a system of classification whereby employers could obtain the services of members accustomed to their particular class of work, and members secured the employment most suitable to their capabilities, failed to find favour when submitted to the consideration of the trade.

A subject which had been discussed on many previous occasions—namely, the long-felt and much-needed want of more commodious premises in which to transact the

Society's business—was at last satisfactorily settled by the Executive announcing that negotiations had been entered into for the purchase of the freehold premises, Nos. 7 and 9, St. Bride Street, which could be secured for the sum of £10,500. An agreement was drawn up and signed in August of 1891, the premises being taken over on the 28th of September. Extensive alterations were designed and commenced during the following year, and on the 30th of January, 1893 (after a thirty-six years' occupation of the house in Racquet Court, during which time the membership had increased fourfold), the Society's business was transferred to the present premises, the event being made memorable by the holding of a Trade Dinner, which took place at the Cannon Street Hotel, on the 28th January.

In reviewing the past history of the Society, it must be a matter of surprise to the members, and particularly to those who, at various periods, were officially connected with the Racquet Court premises, that such a huge quantity of work could have been transacted in so limited a space, especially during later years; and it is certain that the change, from any and every point of view, has been extremely beneficial to all concerned, and has materially assisted to raise the status of the Society as a whole. Apart from higher considerations, and viewing it merely as an investment, the utmost success has attended the purchase, the premises having since been valued at the substantial figure of £15,500—in itself ample testimony to the wisdom of those who selected the building and carried the negotiations for its purchase to a successful issue.

Beyond deciding that the Executive should not be permitted to take a ballot of the trade upon any matter (other than an extension of the Provident Benefit or a grant to another trade society or other body of workers) without calling a Delegate or General Meeting; discussing the propriety of establishing a trade journal; and advancing the salary of the Assistant-Secretary, few matters of general interest engaged the attention of the members during the latter months of 1891. The sum of £500 was granted in December towards the support of the German printers on strike; and early in the following January a Special General Meeting was held by requisition, to "consider what steps should be taken to assist the Bookbinders in their present effort to secure an eight-hour day." A fortnight later a ballot was taken upon the question of the Society "actively supporting the Bookbinders by objecting to work for firms employing Non-Union Binders?" there being but 359 members in favour of such a course of action, those voting against it numbering no less than 6,065. Shortly afterwards, the members granted to the Bookbinders the sum of £100.

In the same month, a Special Delegate Meeting was convened to consider a report from the Trade Committee "as to certain matters that have necessitated the suspension of two of the Society's officers, and to determine what action shall be taken thereon." After fully inquiring into the causes which had led the Committee to reluctantly exercise the powers vested in them by rule, it was determined to declare the position of Assistant Secretary as vacant; the Committee at the same time submitting proposals having for their object the devising of a better method of carrying on the duties hitherto devolving upon that official, rendered necessary by the growth of the Society's membership and the increase of its benefits. No immediate steps were taken to fill the vacant position, the consideration of the matter being deferred until the Annual Meeting in March.

The News Committee, who had instituted an inquiry into the method of working adopted in the various daily paper offices, "with the view of ascertaining whether—and if so, to what extent—irregularities existed, either of scale or custom," reported very fully upon the subject during the month of October, their main recommendation dealing with the manner in which "grass" hands had hitherto been employed. It is also noticeable that the system of presenting printed quarterly and annual reports (instead of in writing) was abandoned by the newsmen within a very short period of its adoption.

Towards the end of 1891, negotiations were entered into with the proprietors of a daily paper into which composing machines had been introduced, with a view to arranging terms for their working; but in spite of every effort on the part of the Executive to arrive at a satisfactory understanding, the negotiations failed, the action of the proprietors in closing the house being vigorously, and, to an extent, successfully resisted.

The year 1892 was destined to witness several changes in the *personnel* of the Executive, Mr. R. W. Minter having, in February, notified the Committee that it was not his intention, "for reasons of a private nature," to seek re-election at the Annual Meeting; this announcement being followed on the 4th of March by a similar declaration from the Secretary (Mr. C. J. Drummond), who, after an official connection with the Society of seventeen years, decided to "hand over the responsibilities of office to his constituents." At the Annual Meeting, held on the 16th of March, the members unanimously adopted a resolution —" That, having learned with regret of the determination of the Secretary not to seek re-election, this Annual Meeting tenders him its very best thanks for the many services he has rendered the Trade, and trusts he may have a bright and happy future."

At this meeting a long discussion ensued upon a proposal to re-open the question affecting the Assistant-Secretaryship, which having been settled by the delegates attending a recently convened Special Meeting, could not, according to Rule, be re-opened within six months. The attempt to override the Rules being persisted in, and a nomination on behalf of the suspended official being handed in (which the Committee declined to accept), the proceedings were brought to a close by the Chairman vacating the chair. The question of adhering to the Rules in this matter was eventually referred to the ballot, the members deciding by 5,956 votes to 1,042 that the decision of the Committee and delegates should be upheld.

The adjourned Meeting was not held until the 30th of March, pending the election of officers, which took place on March 25th. For the position of Chairman, two candidates were nominated, Mr. R. F. McBean being elected by 4,227 votes; the election for the Secretaryship, for which four candidates were nominated, resulting in the return of Mr. C. W. Bowerman (who had previously resigned the News Secretaryship) with 4,135 votes. At the adjourned meeting, three candidates were nominated for the Assistant-Secretaryship, Mr. J. Connal being returned by 3,081 votes. For the position of News Secretary, Mr. T. Sanders was elected by the newsmen.

At the May Delegate Meeting the Trade Committee recommended that in view of the financial position of the Society, it was desirable to permanently increase the subscription to 9d. per week, and to meet all levies for extensions of Provident benefit by levy. The delegates, however, rejected the last proposal, but heartily agreed with the former, their decision being afterwards ratified by a ballot, and by an overwhelming majority. The Executive received instructions to take immediate and energetic steps for the suppression of overtime, "in order to protect the funds of the Society from excessive provident claims," which since 1890 had practically doubled in amount.

Full effect was given to these instructions, a schedule of questions being addressed to the various chapels, requesting the officials to furnish minute particulars as to the quantity and circumstances under which overtime was being worked, and inviting the support of chapels in an endeavour to minimise such work as far as possible. From the information thus received, the Committee found that the increased rates agreed upon at the 1891 Conference "had considerably curtailed the amount of overtime work," which the returns proved had been reduced by at least one-half.

Although the delegates had previously hesitated to accept the principle of "levying" to meet extensions of Provident relief, the bad state of trade in October of 1892 necessitated the calling of a Special Meeting, to consider the "imperative necessity of devising some means whereby the extra expense involved in an extension of benefit could be met," and at this meeting it was decided to grant the extension, and to double the subscription for six weeks, the result of the ballot endorsing this decision by a majority of two to one.

In the preceding August the Executive had received instructions to inquire into the "Gift" question, which for several years had given rise to considerable controversy, and created an acute degree of unpleasantness between member and member. The Committee went very fully into the question, taking evidence from accusers and accused, and in February, 1893, reported that the charges which had been made against the "Gift" societies had been greatly exaggerated, and that the witnesses had failed to substantiate the allegations made at the preceding Delegate Meeting. On the contrary, it was shown that the work and methods of these small organisations had, in some directions, exercised a decidedly beneficial influence upon the well-being of the Society. Whatever might have been the position and power of these minor societies in the past, it was made perfectly clear that by the growth of the parent Society they had been rendered practically ineffective, and had continued to exist solely for provident purposes, for the carrying on of which they still retained the "Call" Book. This the Committee recommended should be abolished, also that the "Gift" membership should be rendered less exclusive —the practice having been to limit the number in each to about 100. The delegates, however, passed a resolution instructing the Executive to appeal to the members constituting "Gifts" to withdraw from such sectional societies, and to "throw the whole of their influence into the general union of London compositors." At the adjourned meeting, the delegates carried a resolution that a ballot should be taken upon the question "Whether the Rules shall be altered to prevent any member of a 'Gift' being a member of the Society," which was carried by a very narrow majority. Since then the members of the "Gifts" have re-constituted their societies in agreement with the desires of the Trade.

Among other subjects discussed at the various meetings had been that of starting a journal in the interests of the London printing trade, the members voting the sum of £30 towards the launching of the "Printing News," the first number of which was published in August, 1892.

At the Annual Meeting in March, 1893, the re-election of the Chairman met with opposition, and, although Mr. McBean obtained the "show of hands," a ballot was demanded on behalf of the two opposing candidates, which resulted in the re-election of the former member.

Accompanying the same ballot paper was a proposal to temporarily extend the Provident Benefit, which was lost by fourteen votes. Following upon this a "Non-Provident Relief Fund" was raised, the appeal (as well as those issued in 1894) being well responded to. The Trade Committee undertook to "exercise a discretionary power" in the distribution of the money subscribed, the task proving a delicate and far from agreeable one. The three appeals realised the sum of £741 4s. 6d.

On Saturday, the 10th of June, 1893, the first of a series of special general meetings was held to take into consideration the Report of a Special Committee appointed in the early part of the preceding year "to consider the desirability of reconstructing the Executive, to meet the continuous growth of the Society ; and that the rights of appeal by individual members be more strictly defined and safeguarded ; also to revise and re-arrange the Rules." At this meeting it was decided to expunge all reference to the News Department, the rules governing which had been revised in the direction of abolishing the separate Executive. Considerable alterations were eventually made in the Society's Rules, the principal being the retirement of members from the Committee after serving for two consecutive periods of twelve months, and to be ineligible for re-election until the expiration of two years ; increasing the subscription to 10d. per week (ratified by ballot) ; fixing the minimum capital at £2 10s. per member ; making fines for non-payment of subscriptions at stated periods cumulative ; and embodying a rule governing the admission of members joining an association "one of whose objects is the procuring of employment for its members." Proposals to increase the strike payment to 30s. per week, to appoint an Organiser, also an additional Assistant, and to increase the salaries of the two Assistants, were rejected.

In consequence of a decision given by the Chairman at the first meeting held to consider the Revised Rules, a requisition was received requesting that a Special General Meeting might be held " to consider the general and special conduct of the Chairman, and the transactions of the General Meeting " held on the 10th of June. Two resolutions accompanied the requisition, the first calling upon the Chairman to resign his position ; the second directing " that any recorded transactions of the General Meeting which may have taken place after the irregular proceedings of the Chairman be deleted from the Minutes." The Committee declined to call a special meeting, and decided to take the discussion of these resolutions as the first business at the adjourned meeting. Upon this occasion an acrimonious discussion arose, but the members eventually endorsed the decisions arrived at at the previous meeting, and proceeded with the consideration of the Revised Rules. As the matters affecting the News Department had been disposed of (for the convenience of whose members the two meetings had been held on a Saturday), it was decided that future meetings should take place on Wednesday evenings ; and upon resuming the consideration of the Special Committee's report upon the 12th of July, a resolution was passed calling upon the Chairman to leave the chair. The Trade Committee, after giving careful consideration to the action of the members, decided to accept their Chairman's resignation, and on the 28th of August, Mr. J. Galbraith was elected to the vacant position.

The News Committee also entered upon the task of revising their Scale, a report being submitted to the members of that department in June, the conclusions arrived at eventually becoming the subject of a Conference with the daily newspaper proprietors, resulting in the laying down of much-needed regulations regarding the charges to be made for displayed and other advertisements, and increasing the guarantee for morning papers to one galley and a half, with several minor but none the less desirable and advantageous alterations.

Several questions of an interesting and important character occupied the attention of the members during the year 1894. At the Annual Meeting, a proposal was submitted and approved that the weekly subscription should be raised to 1s. for a period of twelve months, in order that the capital might be increased to £2 10s. per member, in agreement with the decision of the ballot upon the recommendations of the Special Committee. Reference was also made to the "extraordinary manner in which the Provident claims had increased," and satisfaction expressed at the members' decision to meet all extensions of this benefit by means of a levy.

As an outcome of resolutions which had been passed over-ruling the policy of the Board upon the Apprentice and "Gift" questions, the Committee found it necessary to appeal to the Trade—first, with a view to limiting apprentices to one to three journeymen (instead of, as claimed, one to six), and secondly, to prevent the rule recently passed regarding "members joining associations having for their object the obtaining of employment," being made retrospective so far as "Gift" hands were concerned. It was pointed out that the latter had acquiesced in the reasonable demands which had been made upon them, and that to threaten them with expulsion was both unconstitutional and illegal, and a proceeding which "no Committee, worthy of the name, could tolerate or sympathise with." In each instance the action of the Committee was upheld by a sweeping majority.

Important resolutions were likewise submitted from the unemployed members respecting the propriety of consulting the employers upon the subject of reducing the working hours, and with regard to taking steps to bring about a federation with the Typographical and other Trade Associations. A special meeting was convened for their discussion, and upon submitting the hours question to the ballot, the suggested conference was negatived by 4,167 votes to 2,184. The question of the Society joining the proposed Federation of the Printing and Kindred Trades in London was likewise balloted upon, 3,653 members opposing and 2,646 approving such a course of action. Over 9,000 papers were issued to members, nearly one-third of whom failed to record their votes.

GOVERNMENT PRINTING CONTRACTS.

In August, an interesting debate was raised in the House of Commons with respect to the Contracts for Government printing, upon a motion brought forward by Mr. T. Lough (Member for West Islington) during the discussion on the Estimates. The question had been taken up by the Trade Committee towards the close of the preceding year, and in November a deputation obtained an interview with Mr. T. D. Pigott (Controller of the Stationery Office), to whom was explained the difference between the prices embodied in the official Schedules and those in the London Scale of Prices, the Controller being urged to introduce into future tenders a condition insisting that the Contractor should pay his workmen in agreement with the provisions of the recognised Scale. At a later date, an interview was obtained with Sir William Harcourt (Chancellor of the Exchequer) and Sir John T. Hibbert (Secretary to the Treasury), followed by a second interview with the Controller of the Stationery Office.

The matter was then entrusted to Mr. T. Lough, who very kindly, and with the utmost readiness, consented to undertake the task. Very quickly (in conjunction with Mr. S. Woods) an interview was arranged with the Secretary to the Treasury, with whom was the Controller of the Stationery Office, and after hearing the representations placed before him by the deputation, the former admitted that a strong case had been made out, which should receive his careful consideration. The result, however, of the Treasury Secretary's deliberations was not so satisfactory as could be desired, and Mr. Lough took the opportunity of raising the subject in the House, as stated above. His efforts received valuable support at the hands of Mr. Michael Austin, Sir Albert Rollit, Mr. J. Stuart, Captain Norton, and Mr. John Burns, and finally the Secretary to the Treasury agreed to the appointment of a Select Committee to inquire into the matter, and that, pending the report of the Committee, any new contracts that might be entered into should be given only to firms agreeing to pay the London Scale of Prices to their compositors.

This Committee (which was appointed on the 18th of June, 1895) met on the 21st of the same month, elected a Chairman, and arranged to meet during the following week to take evidence. Meanwhile, however, the Liberal Government met with a defeat, and resigned ; and it was not until the 25th of February, 1896, that the Committee was re-appointed, the change of Government naturally involving changes in its constitution, in agreement with the political views of the party in power. The Chairman was re-elected, and after it had been decided that the question of establishing a State printing office was outside the scope of the Committee's inquiry (this decision causing the retirement of two of its members), evidence was taken on the 6th of March, and occupied nine sittings (until the 24th of April).

On the 8th of May, the Chairman's report was rejected in favour of the report presented by Mr. Lough, and, after agreeing to many of its paragraphs, the Committee adjourned until the 13th of May, when one of its members who, although a supporter of the Government, had not previously taken the trouble to attend any of its meetings, and who, consequently, had not heard the evidence upon which the Committee had to base its report, attended for the first time, apparently as a matter of political exigency ; and as by his presence the Committee became equally divided in opinion, the Chairman was enabled to give his casting vote against the main recommendations embodied in Mr. Lough's report.

In spite, however, of the political bias which had been imported into the proceedings, the Committee's recommendations were considerably in advance of those resulting from former inquiries, and in addition to inserting in the form of contract regulations governing sweating, sub-letting, and the payment of wages, the Report advised that "the various groups of printing should be so distributed as to ensure a healthy competition." The result has been that whereas a large proportion of Government printing was formerly monopolised by a non-society house, most of it has now been secured by firms recognizing and honourably abiding by the Scale of Prices mutually agreed upon between, and signed by, the representatives of employers and employed, the consequent effect upon the recognized trade in general, and upon the members of the Society in particular, being extremely beneficial so far as their present and future welfare is concerned.

In order that the members might be afforded an opportunity of expressing their appreciation of the services rendered to the Trade by Messrs. T. Lough and M. Austin, a Complimentary Dinner was given in their honour at the Holborn Restaurant, on February 20th, 1897, which was attended by representatives from the Provincial Typographical Association and other kindred societies. On this occasion handsome illuminated addresses (in album form) were presented to the gentlemen mentioned, conveying the feelings entertained towards them by those whose interests they had so well served.

In September of 1894, a ballot was taken upon the question of reducing the subscription payable by unemployed members to 4d. per week, the trade upholding, by an exceedingly large majority, the principle that whilst members enjoyed equal rights and privileges they must bear an equal liability.

The delegates attending the August quarterly meeting appointed a Special Committee of three to " consider the Sub-Committees of the Executive, with a view to abolishing a considerable and unnecessary drain upon our funds." This Committee reported to the November meeting, submitting seven recommendations, some of which were accepted by the delegates, and have since been carried into effect.

On the 6th of April, 1895, the subscription was permanently increased to 1s. per week ; and by the same ballot it was almost unanimously decided to discontinue the Library—a course which the Committee regretfully advised the Trade to take in consequence of the extremely limited number of borrowers availing themselves of its advantages. At a later period the whole of the books (with the exception of the works of reference) were sold by auction to the members.

At the May Delegate Meeting, the Committee submitted a proposal dealing with the question of reinstituting a system of half-provident benefit to members drawing three-fourths of the maximum amount of relief for three successive years, but the recommendation was rejected, and a Special Committee of five appointed to " devise the best means of decreasing the number of unemployed members." This Committee reported in August, their recommendations (eight in number) being submitted to the votes of members during the following month. A proposal that no member be allowed to work overtime while other members were to be obtained from the Society House was rejected; as also were the proposals to appoint an Organiser, an Admission Committee, a Committee to inquire into the seasonal nature of the trade, and to provide telephonic communication with employers. The proposals approved were those dealing with boy labour, "high-pressure" production, and federation with the Typographical Association.

An important question was also referred to the members from the August Delegate Meeting, having reference to the resolution passed at the Trade Union Congress, held at Norwich in 1894, and known as the "Collectivist" Resolution, the rescinding of which was to be proposed at the Congress to be held during the following month. By 3,157 votes to 2,193, the members decided to instruct their delegates attending the Cardiff Congress to support the motion to rescind the resolution in question. The Society's delegates to the Trade Union Congress were this year, for the first time, elected by ballot.

MACHINE COMPOSING QUESTION.

Although an agreement had been arrived at in August, 1892, regarding the prices and conditions under which type-distributing and composing machines should be worked in a daily paper office (the negotiations in connection therewith being memorable on account of the attempt then made to introduce girl and boy labour for distributing purposes—an attempt which the Society strenuously and successfully resisted), it was not until 1894 that the question of fixing rates for line-casting machines was raised by the proprietors of the daily papers, to whom a memorial had been presented by the newsmen regarding advertisement and other charges. A Conference upon the subject was held at Anderton's Hotel, and on the 7th of June a Scale was drawn up and signed, and made binding upon all parties until the end of 1895.

In November of that year, the employers announced their intention of re-opening the question at the expiration of the agreed-upon time, and another Conference was consequently convened at Anderton's Hotel, at which a strong effort was made by their representatives to force a general and serious reduction of the prices hitherto prevailing. This attempt was in the main frustrated, after a persistent and long-sustained struggle ; but when the terms provisionally agreed upon were submitted to the trade, the members referred them back for further consideration, and eventually a committee was appointed to carry on further negotiations with the employers.

On the 25th of January, 1896, a Special General Meeting was held at Exeter Hall to consider the position created by the rejection of the provisional terms of agreement. The proceedings were throughout marked with considerable enthusiasm, it being agreed that no compromise should be accepted, and that, pending the discussion of fresh terms, the employers should be called upon to recognise the existing machine scale, the members also deciding to pay a substantial levy for a period of six weeks. In February, a Special Committee was appointed "to re-cast the scale," and to arrange working conditions between case hands and operators. During the same month one of the daily paper offices was unfortunately closed to the members through a dispute in connection with the conditions under which machines were to be worked.

In June, another Conference was convened with the employers' representatives, which took place at the Salisbury Hotel, Salisbury Square, and after several sittings had been devoted to the discussion of the points in dispute, an Agreement was signed on the 27th of July, which came into operation on the 1st of September following. A condition of meeting the employers in conference was that the Society's Representatives should have power to sign the terms agreed upon, this course being approved by the members by 4,753 votes to 1,508. The Scale worked with an agreeable degree of smoothness until towards the end of 1897, when minor questions arose in connection with the interpretation of certain of the Rules, which for the moment proved difficult of settlement; but, as the result of a meeting of the Arbitration Board (called together in agreement with resolutions passed at the previous Conference, and which were appended to the Scale), these matters were satisfactorily disposed of, the decisions arrived at being embodied in a Minute signed on the 25th of January, 1898.

With the exception of the Machine question, which engrossed the attention of the members to the exclusion of other than the ordinary routine business, very few matters arose in 1896 which require to be chronicled. The Society was represented at the International Workers' Congress, held in London during the month of July, which was very largely attended by foreign delegates, and afforded English trade-unionists ample opportunities of ascertaining the views of Continental workmen upon the various labour and social questions discussed at the Congress. Advantage was taken of the presence of representatives from the Typographical Federations of France, Spain, and other countries, to invite them to a banquet, the delegates expressing the warmest sentiments of appreciation of the hospitality extended towards them by the Society.

Towards the close of the year, a serious dispute occurred between Lord Penrhyn and the North Wales quarrymen, who struck in defence of "the right of combination." The struggle was maintained by the men in the most stubborn and determined manner, and extended over many months, during which period they received and retained the unstinted support of the general public, as well as the hearty co-operation of their fellow trade-unionists, of whom the members of this Society contributed from their funds the sum of £350, very large additional amounts being subscribed through the various chapels.

A scheme of Federation between the Society and the London Machine Managers' Society was formulated about this time, and accepted by the latter body, but upon being submitted to the Delegate Meeting held in February, 1897, was referred back to the Committee for further consideration, the members feeling that the scheme was not sufficiently wide in its scope. Negotiations were opened up with the kindred trades of the Metropolis, and eventually another scheme was drawn up, which, after meeting with the approval of the delegates attending the November meeting, was submitted to a ballot, and endorsed by 4,976 votes to 1,362. The members of the Machine Managers' Society have not at present decided to join this Federation.

The year 1897 also witnessed the commencement of the unsuccessful struggle of the members of the Amalgamated Society of Engineers to secure "an eight-hour working day." To assist them to accomplish this desirable object, a meeting was convened by the Society at Exeter Hall, in order that public sympathy might be enlisted on the side of the engineers; the members also subscribing the sum of £60 per week towards their support, besides levying themselves to the extent of 3*d.* per member per week, the total sum thus subscribed by grants and levies amounting to over £3,139.

It will be agreed that no more fitting action could have been taken by the members than that which was decided upon within a few days of the close of the year, namely, that in order to commemorate the fiftieth anniversary of the Society's re-establishment, the allowances paid to the Superannuated members should be increased all round, the maximum payment being raised to 10*s.* per week for members totally incapacitated, with a minimum payment of 5*s.* per week for those partially incapacitated. The feeling of the Trade upon the subject is best expressed by the result of the ballot, 6,414 members voting in favour of the proposed increases, and but 134 in the negative. At the close of the financial year there were 123 members upon the Superannuation Fund, each of whom received the benefit of the increased scale of payments from the 1st of January, 1898.

AMOUNTS EXPENDED IN BENEFITS, 1848-1898.

UNEMPLOYED ALLOWANCES.

With the re-establishment of the Society in 1848, a Voluntary Provident Fund was started, the subscription to which was 2*d*. per week, entitling unemployed members to 8*s*. per week during a period of fifteen weeks, the Fund being subsidised by the Society to the extent of one-fourth of its income, such grant not to exceed the sum of £200 per annum. In 1863, the Provident Fund was incorporated with the Trade Society, the benefit still remaining at 8*s*. per week, for thirteen weeks only; in 1866, the relief was increased to 10*s*. per week, and in August of 1879 to 12*s*. per week, the maximum payment being fixed at £9 12*s*. per year, extending over a period of sixteen weeks.

PAYMENTS TO UNEMPLOYED MEMBERS.

During five years		An average per year of	Membership at end of period.
1848-1852	£982 13 1	£196 10 7	2,100
1853-1857	1,315 9 0	263 1 9	2,250
1858-1862	2,459 3 11	491 16 9	2,175
1863-1867	7,378 7 4	1,475 13 5	3,290
1868-1872	12,005 16 5	2,201 3 3	3,700
1873-1877	7,980 3 10	1,596 0 9	4,795
1878-1882	23,365 16 3	4,673 3 3	5,660
1883-1887	23,599 3 8	4,719 16 9	7,025
1888-1892	38,816 18 7	7,763 7 8	9,798
1893-1897	61,079 10 11	12,215 18 2	10,780
	£178,983 3 0		

An average expenditure of £3,579 13*s*. 3*d*. per year.

TRAVELLING ALLOWANCES.

Members leaving London in 1848 to seek work in the provinces were entitled to receive with their travelling cards the sum of 5s. as a gift, with a further sum of 5s. as a loan, the former also to be repaid in the event of the member returning within three months. Country compositors holding travelling cards were also relieved to the extent of 5s. After 1857 the loan benefit was deleted from the Rules; and in 1871 members of six months' standing received a gift of 10s.; twelve months, 15s.; two years, 20s.; three years, 25s.; four years, 30s.; five years and upwards, 35s. These allowances were afterwards reduced to nearly half these amounts, the minimum payment being 5s. and the maximum 20s. In 1881, the payments were again increased, and became known as Removal Grants; and in 1890 the maximum benefit was fixed at 45s.

PAYMENTS TO TRAVELLING MEMBERS.

During five years			An average per year
1848–1852	...	£212 4 0	£42 8 10
1853–1857	...	249 12 3	49 18 5
1858–1862	...	351 15 2	70 7 0
1863–1867	...	343 9 2	68 13 10
1868–1872	...	696 10 6	139 6 1
1873–1877	...	434 10 6	86 18 1
1878–1882	...	329 16 0	65 19 2
1883–1887	...	366 0 0	73 4 0
1888–1892	...	923 10 0	184 14 0
1893–1897	...	1,770 5 0	354 1 0
		£5,677 12 7	

An average expenditure of £113 11s. per year.

EMIGRATION GRANTS.

This benefit was first established in 1853, at a time when the "rush" for Australia had set in. It was in the nature of an "advance," the business of the Emigration Aid Society being conducted by a Committee appointed by the members, the Society making certain annual grants towards carrying out the object in view. From 1853 to 1857, the sum of £800 was advanced from the funds. The benefit then appears to have been discontinued until 1871, when it was again embodied in the Society's Rules, with a maximum allowance of £10, and a restricted expenditure to the extent of £300 per year. Since 1890, however, the maximum grant has been increased to £15.

AMOUNTS DRAWN BY EMIGRANT MEMBERS.

From		An average per year of
1853–1857	£800 0 0	... £160 0 0
1871–1872	345 14 0	... 69 0 0
1873–1877	674 16 10	... 134 19 4
1878–1882	979 12 0	... 195 18 7
1883–1887	1,054 0 0	... 210 16 0
1888–1892	1,070 0 0	... 214 0 0
1893–1897	983 11 8	... 196 14 4
	£5,907 14 6	

An average expenditure for the 31 years of £190 11s. 5d. per year.

GRANTS TO MEDICAL INSTITUTIONS.

The first grant under the heading of Medical Charities was made in 1858, since which period they have increased in amount from 14 guineas to 266 guineas per annum, and will doubtless increase with the growth of the membership.

ANNUAL GRANTS.

From					An average per year of
1858-1862	...	£190 1 0	...	£38 0 2
1863-1867	...	379 1 0	...	75 16 2
1868-1872	...	480 18 0	...	96 3 7
1873-1877	...	696 3 0	...	139 4 7
1878-1882	...	756 0 0	...	151 4 0
1883-1887	...	782 5 0	...	156 9 0
1888-1892	...	1,174 10 0	...	234 18 0
1893-1897	...	1,292 0 0	...	258 5 0
		£5,750 18 0		

An average expenditure of about £115 per year.

FUNERAL ALLOWANCES.

No provision of this character was incorporated in the Society's Rules until 1868, when it was decided that at the death of a member of five years' standing the sum of £5 should be paid to his representatives, with a further sum of £1 for each additional year's membership until a maximum payment of £12 was reached. In 1874 the minimum payment was fixed at £4 (after three years' membership), and the maximum at £15.

AMOUNTS PAID IN FUNERAL ALLOWANCES.

From					An average per year of
1868-1872	...	£1,692 7 0	...	£338 9 5
1873-1877	...	2,954 0 1	...	590 16 0
1878-1882	...	4,594 12 4	...	918 18 5
1883-1887	...	5,233 13 4	...	1,046 14
1888-1892	...	7,497 16 0	...	1,499 11 2
1893-1897	...	8,257 15 7	...	1,651 11 1
		£30,230 4 4		

An average expenditure during the 30 years of £1,007 13s. 5d. per year.

SUPERANNUATION ALLOWANCES.

This important benefit, which was embodied in the Society's Rules in September, 1874, came into operation in the year 1877, when eight members were placed upon the fund, each of whom (with one exception) were receiving the sum of 5s. per week, the maximum benefit being 10s. per week after 30 years' membership. For some time the progress of this benefit was watched with considerable interest, both by the various Executives as well as by the members, and in 1881 it was determined (on account of the heavy expenditure) to reduce the maximum allowance to 6s. per week. In 1889 this was increased to 8s., and at the close of 1897 to 10s. per week.

PAYMENTS TO SUPERANNUATED MEMBERS.

From			No. on fund at end of period.
1877-1882	...	£2,872 18 0	56
1883-1887	...	5,101 1 0	94
1888-1892	...	6,541 8 0	113
1893-1897	...	9,374 8 6	123
		£23,889 15 6	

An average expenditure for the 21 years of £1,137 12s. 2d. per year.

LAW AND DEFENCE OF SCALE.

The expenditure under this heading has necessarily been of a more or less fluctuating character, controlled but indirectly by the growth of the membership. The totals set forth include payments to strike hands, compensation to members losing employment through various causes (principally in connection with the maintenance of the Scale) and in recognition of "missionary" work, as well as solicitors' fees.

PAYMENTS TO STRIKE HANDS, ETC.

From					An average per year of		
1848-1852	£231	14	9	...	£46	6	11
1853-1857	834	8	2	...	166	17	7
1858-1862	1,227	18	8	...	245	11	8
1863-1867	1,602	18	6	...	320	11	8
1868-1872	7,187	2	4	...	1,637	8	5
1873-1877	2,096	14	4	...	419	6	10
1878-1882	3,541	8	9	...	708	5	9
1883-1887	4,507	11	7	...	901	10	3
1888-1892	4,428	6	5	...	885	15	3
1893-1897	5,154	17	0	...	1,030	19	5
	£30,813	0	6				

An average expenditure of £616 5s. 2d. per year.

Separating the items comprised in the above total, the following results are shown:—

Payments to Strike Hands	£24,052	13	2
,, as Compensation	2,078	11	8
,, for Missionary Work ...	941	15	8
Solicitors' Fees, etc.	3,740	0	0
	£30,813	0	6

FIRE CLAIMS.

From					An average per year of		
1852-1862	£93	12	0	...	£8	11	2
1863-1867	8	10	6	...	1	14	1
1868-1872	25	18	5	...	5	3	8
1873-1877	64	0	8	...	12	16	1
1878-1882	118	10	3	...	23	14	0
1883-1887	164	18	1	...	32	19	7
1888-1892	128	1	6	...	25	12	3
1893-1897	167	15	6	...	33	11	1
	£771	6	11				

An average expenditure for the 46 years of £16 15s. 4d. per year.

TOTAL SUM EXPENDED IN BENEFITS.

Unemployed Allowances	£178,983	3 0
Travelling ,,	5,677	12 7
Emigration ,,	5,907	14 6
Funeral ,,	30,230	4 4
Superannuation ,,	23,889	15 6
Grants to Medical Charities	5,750	18 0
Law and Defence of Scale	30,813	0 6
Fire Claims	771	6 11
	£282,023	15 4

First Annual Balance Sheet of the London Society of Compositors (for the year 1848).

INCOME.	£	s.	d.
Quarterly Subscriptions, Book Department ...	676	0	0
,, ,, News* ...	87	14	1
By Sale of Scales and Reports ...	5	12	6
,, Waste Paper ...	2	1	8
From Provident Fund for Officers' Services, etc.	17	15	6
Balance in hand at end of 1848 ...	39	2	0½

EXPENDITURE.	£	s.	d.
Paid to Unemployed, Balance due on last year	113	3	6
,, Strike-hands, ,, ,,	101	11	1
Paid for Hire of Rooms for General and Delegated Meetings ...	8	2	0
,, Hire of Rooms at "Falcon" Tavern ...	30	0	0
,, Doorkeepers at Meetings ...	1	2	6
,, Committee and Auditors' Expenses ...	34	0	0
,, Delivering Notices, Stationery, Postage, etc. ...	9	17	4
,, Printing Account ...	20	3	0
,, Officers' Salaries ...	118	10	0
,, Tramps, at 5s. each ...	36	0	0
,, Members, on Account of Disputes ...	27	4	5
Paid to Provident Fund, one-fourth Receipts ...	78	4	4½
News Department, Expenses of ...	14	8	7
	592	6	9½
In hands of Messrs. Child & Co., Bankers, at end of 1848 ...	235	19	0

Annual Financial Circular for 1897.

Receipts.

	£	s.	d.
In hand	8,753	7	0½
Contributions:—			
Book Department—			
First Quarter £5,891 5 4			
Second ,, ... 6,089 1 6			
Third ,, ... 5,564 14 4			
Fourth ,, ... 6,090 3 7			
	23,635	4	9
News Department—			
First Quarter £802 16 0			
Second ,, ... 903 0 4			
Third ,, ... 841 17 9			
Fourth ,, ... 897 4 0			
	3,444	18	1
Entrance Fees	343	14	0
Fines	159	17	8
Returned Removal Allowances	38	9	6
,, Emigration ,,	25	7	6
,, Provident ,,	4	3	5
,, Advances	1	4	9
Benefit Deposits	5	5	0
Rent—Cooper, Dennison and Walkden	390	0	0
,, Permanent Sick Fund	6	5	0
Hire of Board Room	18	17	6
Interest on Investments—			
Harrogate £42 1 0			
Torquay 82 16 4			
Barry 83 9 10			
Poole 54 14 6			
Wakefield 42 1 0			
Gloucester 55 13 8			
Penzance 55 2 0			
Widnes 54 13 4			
Cambridge 27 13 11			
Interest on Loans—			
Hackney 111 17 6			
Farringdon Street 30 18 8			
Settles Street 48 6 8			
Upcerne Road 35 5 8			
	724	14	1
Trade Emblems (35 at 2s.)	3	10	0
Scales (525 at 6d.)	13	2	6
Compositors' Guides (1,046 at 2d.)	8	14	4
Typographical Ready Reckoners (40 at 3d.)	0	10	0
Petition Books (31 at 1s.)	1	11	0
Invitation Cards (19 at 6d.)	0	9	6
By Sale of Library Fittings	2	10	0
,, Excursion	147	9	9
,, Levies for Engineers	868	0	0
	£38,597	5	4½

Expenditure.

	£	s.	d.
Unemployed Allowances (1,922 recipients)	10,080	16	5
Superannuation ,, (142 ,,)	2,027	19	0
Funeral ,, (166 ,,)	1,554	6	8
Emigration ,, (19 ,,)	175	0	0
Removal ,, (103 ,,)	183	10	0
Fire ,, (25 ,,)	9	8	7
Advances	4	15	0
Law and Defence of Scale:—			
Strike Hands £153 6 1			
Compensation 155 17 0			
Missionary Work 17 8 0			
Reporters' Fees 2 9 4			
Solicitors' Bill of Costs (1896) 80 13 10			
	409	14	3
Committees	272	0	0
Deputations	16	19	6
Ballot Scrutineers	60	6	0
Printing	493	8	9
Stationery	29	6	11
Coal £15 0 0			
Electric Light 69 10 8			
Fire Insurance 27 0 0			
Gas 0 1 8			
Hire of Halls 105 15 6			
Income Tax 37 10 0			
Rates and Taxes 111 9 2			
Water 10 10 0			
	376	17	0
Guarantee Society	6	0	0
Medical Certificates	9	1	6
Returned Benefit Deposits	3	12	0
,, Entry Fees	6	15	0
,, Subscriptions	1	17	11
London Trades' Council	120	1	1
St. Bride Street Property	63	3	2
Scottish Circulars	4	6	4
Medical Charities	279	6	0
Trade ,,	31	10	0
Caxton Convalescent Home	30	0	0
Trades Union Congress and Reports	41	10	11
Zurich Congress	15	0	0
Lough-Austin Dinner and Testimonial	81	9	6
Grants to Engineers	780	0	0
Levies for ,,	868	0	0
Penrhyn Quarrymen	340	0	0
Grants to various Societies, &c.	91	13	0
Addressing Envelopes and Wrappers	7	3	0
Postage and Telegrams	81	19	4
Newspapers and Magazines	54	14	0
Bookbinding	2	6	0
Advanced for Emblem Frames	3	15	0
News Department—			
Committees £113 16 0			
Witnesses 4 19 0			
Deputations 5 0 0			
Delegate to Book Dept. 4 10 0			
Printing 7 13 6			
Stationery 1 1 4			
Ballot Scrutiny 2 2 0			
Auditors 1 10 0			
Grant to Housekeeper 1 0 0			
Postage 1 9 9			
Secretary (special vote) 20 0 0			
Hire of Hall 5 5 0			
Compensation 40 0 0			
Secretary's Salary 30 0 0			
	238	12	7
Salaries	678	4	4
Mrs. Self's Allowance	50	0	0
Housekeeper's ,,	81	0	0
House Expenses	14	17	4
Auditors' Fees	10	16	0
Trustees' ,,	3	7	6
Accountants' Charges for 1896	72	19	0
Miscellaneous	25	11	8
By Investments	8,002	8	6
,, Excursion	142	18	11
,, Superannuation and Funeral Account	1,140	6	9
,, Cash at Bank £9,427 5 3			
,, ,, in hand 81 3 0½			
	9,508	8	3½
	£38,597	5	4½

LONDON SOCIETY OF COMPOSITORS.

Total State of the Society's Funds.
December 25th, 1897.

		£ s. d.	£ s. d.
CAPITAL ACCOUNT:			
By Loans—			
5 % Hackney Loan	£2,500 0 0		
5 % Settles Street Loan	1,000 0 0		
5 % Upcerne Road Loan	730 0 0		
4 % Farringdon Street Loan	800 0 0		
3 % Pontefract Rural Council Loan..	4,000 0 0		
		9,030 0 0	
,, Investments—			
3 % Torquay Corporation Redeemable Stock	£1,976 1 0		
3 % Wakefield ,, ,, ,,	1,508 6 0		
3 % Harrogate ,, ,, ,,	1,517 2 3		
3 % Barry ,, ,, ,,	2,001 13 0		
3 % Poole ,, ,, ,,	2,000 7 9		
3 % Penzance ,, ,, ,,	1,999 16 0		
3 % Widnes ,, ,, ,,	1,998 3 3		
3 % Cambridge ,, ,, ,,	2,000 15 6		
3 % Gloucester ,, ,, ,,	2,001 13 0		
		17,003 17 9	
,, Cash at Bank (including £212 3s. 5d. to be transferred to Superannuation Account)..	£9,427 5 3		
,, Cash in hand	81 3 0½		
		9,508 8 3½	
			35,542 6 0½
SUPERANNUATION AND FUNERAL ACCOUNT:—			
By Investments—			
3 % Torquay Corporation Redeemable Stock		1,000 0 0	
3 % Barry ,, ,, ,,		1,000 0 0	
3 % Pontefract Rural Council Loan.. ,,		1,000 0 0	
,, Cash at Bank		500 1 0	
			3,500 1 0
ªFREEHOLD PROPERTY, ST. BRIDE STREET			15,500 0 0
Increase on the Year	£9,897 16s 6d.		**£54,542 7 0½**

ªThis amount is exclusive of the value of Furniture and Fittings, which are insured for £1,000.

Number of Members, 10,780.

We hereby certify that we have examined the above statement of the Society's Funds, and the Securities for the respective Loans, and have verified the Certificates of Investments, together with the Balances at the Bankers and in hand, and in our opinion it is a correct statement thereof.

Dated this 2nd day of February, 1898.   WARD & WILDING, *Chartered Accountants*,
2, Clement's Inn, W.C.

PETITION FUND ACCOUNT.*
From 26th December, 1896, to 25th December, 1897.

Receipts.	£ s. d.	Expenditure.	£ s. d.
In hand, Dec. 26th, 1896	54 10 6	Paid over during the year	353 16 4
Cash received during year	384 13 1	Balance in hand, Dec. 25th, 1897	85 7 3
	£439 3 7		£439 3 7

* This Account is audited monthly by the Finance Committee.

We have examined the Petition Fund Account, and compared it with the Books and Vouchers thereof, and certify that it is correct and in accordance therewith.

Dated this 2nd day of February, 1898.   WARD & WILDING, *Chartered Accountants*,
2, Clement's Inn, W.C

SUPERANNUATION AND FUNERAL ACCOUNT.
From 26th December, 1896, to 25th December, 1897.

Receipts.	£ s. d.	Expenditure.	£ s. d.
In hand, Dec. 25th, 1896	725 19 7	By Pontefract Rural Loan	1,000 0 0
Interest	55 8 0	,, Superannuation Allowances	2,027 19 0
Amount set off from Contributions during the year	4,513 2 6½	,, Funeral	1,554 6 2
		Cash at Bank £500 1 0	
		,, to be received from General Account, and being part of the amount of £9,427 5 3 at Bank, as mentioned above 212 3 5½	712 4 5½
	£5,294 10 1½		£5,294 10 1½

Table showing the average Expenditure for the various Benefits of the Society, from 1848 to 1897.

Year.	Members.	Strike. Yearly Amount. £ s. d.	Strike. Avge. per Member.	Unemployed. Yearly Amount. £ s. d.	Unemployed. Avge. per Member.	Emigration. Yearly Amount. £ s. d.	Emigration. Avge. per Member.	Travelling. Yearly Amount. £ s. d.	Travelling. Avge. per Member.
1848	1100	128 16 6	2 4	186 2 10	3 4½	250 0 0	1 11	36 0 0	0 7¾
1849	1500	16 7 5	0 2½	187 18 5	2 6	350 0 0	2 11¾	51 5 0	0 8
1850	1800	7 1 6	0 0¾	200 0 0	2 2½	100 0 0	0 10½	43 5 0	0 5¾
1851	1950	11 14 0	0 1½	176 1 1	1 9½	100 0 0	1 0	50 4 0	0 6
1852	2100	67 15 4	0 7¾	232 10 9	7 2½	...	...	31 10 0	0 3½
1853	2000	11 18 0	0 1	94 12 3	0 8¾	...	...	29 5 0	0 2½
1854	2350	28 10 4	0 2¾	51 12 6	0 5¼	...	...	40 7 0	0 4
1855	2300	25 14 11	0 2½	730 12 2	6 4	...	...	38 11 6	0 4
1856	2000	63 9 3	0 7½	238 12 1	2 4½	...	...	76 2 0	0 9
1857	2250	704 15 8	6 3	200 0 0	1 9¼	...	...	65 6 9	0 0¾
1858	2600	540 16 5	4 1¾	346 12 11	2 7¾	...	...	63 11 2	0 5¾
1859	2550	70 16 9	0 6½	200 0 0	1 6¾	...	...	66 13 0	0 6¼
1860	2050	289 1 2	2 2	200 0 0	1 6	...	...	44 2 0	0 3¾
1861	2550	5 8 2	0 0½	1034 12 11	8 1¼	...	...	75 19 6	0 7
1862	2170	321 16 2	2 11½	677 18 1	6 2¾	...	...	101 9 6	0 11
1863	2555	308 8 2	2 4¾	393 19 5	3 1	...	...	68 1 0	0 6¼
1864	2600	243 14 4	1 10½	1064 14 11	8 2¼	...	...	61 1 2	0 5½
1865	2800	98 16 1	0 8	1633 14 0	11 8	...	...	57 6 6	0 4¾
1866	3335	174 19 10	1 0½	1800 9 10	10 9½	...	...	64 19 0	0 4½
1867	3200	777 0 1	4 8¾	2485 9 2	15 1¼	...	...	92 1 6	0 6½
1868	3320	549 4 4	3 2½	2317 9 6	13 0½	...	...	70 11 6	0 5
1869	3300	448 10 7	2 8½	2086 7 1	16 3¼	...	...	86 12 6	0 6¼
1870	3350	1815 10 8	10 10	3917 0 9	23 4½	...	...	91 14 6	0 6½
1871	3500	303 14 1	1 8¾	1822 8 9	10 4¼	113 0 0	0 7½	232 17 0	1 3¾
1872	3700	4070 2 8	22 0	1262 10 4	6 9¾	232 14 0	1 3	214 15 0	1 1¾
1873	3700	493 11 8	2 6	1095 10 5	5 11	191 0 0	1 0½	80 17 6	0 5
1874	3800	640 10 9	3 4½	1258 13 11	6 7½	203 10 1	1 0¾	90 15 0	0 5½
1875	4200	88 2 3	0 5	848 7 11	4 0¼	122 0 0	0 6¾	84 0 6	0 4¾
1876	4445	659 8 11	2 11½	2225 17 7	10 0	103 6 9	0 5½	80 9 0	0 4½
1877	4450	245 0 9	1 1	2551 14 0	11 4½	55 0 0	0 2¾	98 9 0	0 5¼
1878	4700	362 10 5	1 6½	3263 18 2	13 10½	73 1 0	0 3½	102 12 0	0 5
1879	4900	1700 11 4	6/10	5318 2 6	21 6¾	271 9 4	1 1	63 19 6	0 3
1880	5100	229 12 10	0/10¾	4997 17 0	19 7	196 1 8	0 9	66 11 6	0 3
1881	5300	534 9 6	2 0	4985 3 3	18 9½	231 0 0	0 10½	50 8 0	0 2¼
1882	5600	711 15 8	2 6¾	4800 15 4	16 11½	208 0 0	0 8¾	37 5 0	0 1½
1883	5850	661 0 2	2 3	4140 3 11	14 0	219 0 0	0 8¾	69 0 0	0 2¾
1884	6175	575 16 1	1/10½	4005 6 10	12 11½	201 0 0	0 7¾	54 10 0	0 2
1885	6415	1202 11 2	3 8¾	5267 17 11	16 4¼	191 0 0	0 7	114 0 0	0 4
1886	6555	1325 0 2	4 0¼	5442 4 2	16 7¼	266 0 0	0 9½	53 0 0	0 1¾
1887	7025	743 4 0	2 0½	4743 10 10	13 6	177 0 0	0 6	75 10 0	0 2½
1888	7400	459 1 2	1 2¾	5544 6 5	14 11¾	150 0 0	0 4¾	60 15 0	0 1¾
1889	7655	624 12 0	1 6¼	5168 11 5	13 0½	285 0 0	0 8½	80 0 0	0 2½
1890	[illegible]	[illegible] 8 2	1 2	5549 0 9	12 5	138 0 0	0 4¼	88 0 0	0 2¾
1891	9350	1715 4 11	3 8	10038 13 8	22 0	175 0 0	0 4½	321 15 0	0 8¼
1892	9792	1104 0 2	2 3	11000 6 4	24 3¾	119 0 0	0 7¾	367 0 0	0 9
1893	10151	1666 4 0	3 3¾	11865 11 6	23 4½	209 0 0	0 7	305 15 0	0 9¼
1894	10011	1196 19 3½	2 4¾	16583 13 1	33 1½	214 0 0	0 5	516 15 0	1 0½
1895	10280	890 15 10	1 8¾	11940 18 0	23 2½	168 11 8	0 4	361 5 0	0 8½
1896	10558	901 1 8	1 10½	10618 11 5	20 1¼	128 0 0	0 1	311 0 0	0 7
1897	10780	400 14 3	0 9	10080 10 5	18 8¼	175 0 0	0 1	183 10 0	0 4

Year.	Superannuation. Yearly Amount. £ s. d.	Superannuation. Avge. per Member.	Funerals. Yearly Amount. £ s. d.	Funerals. Avge. per Member.	Fire. Yearly Amount. £ s. d.	Fire. Avge. per Member.	Grants. Yearly Amount. £ s. d.	Grants. Avge. per Member.	Management. Yearly Amount. £ s. d.	Management. Avge. per Member.	Funds. Yearly Amount. £ s. d.	Funds. Avge. per Member.
1848	...	...	...	...	...	...	...	...	236 2 5	4 3½	235 19 0	0 4 3¼
1849	...	...	...	...	...	...	62 6 0	0 9¾	233 8 6	3 1¼	488 16 0	0 6 3¾
1850	...	...	...	...	...	...	40 0 0	0 5¼	249 1 0	2 9	984 14 10	0 10 11¼
1851	...	...	...	...	...	...	145 0 0	1 5¾	348 9 3	3 10¼	1420 4 7	0 14 6¾
1852	...	...	...	...	4 18 6	0 2¼	135 0 0	1 3¼	316 17 6	3 0	1862 15 5	0 17 8¾
1853	...	...	...	...	62 6 9	0 5¾	10 0 0	0 0¾	744 19 7	5 8¾	2253 11 3	0 17 4
1854	...	...	...	...	...	...	485 0 0	4 1½	427 13 7	3 7½	2447 16 3	1 0 9¾
1855	...	...	...	...	...	...	...	...	884 13 9	7 8¼	2270 3 7	0 19 8¾
1856	...	...	...	...	...	...	...	...	871 3 10	8 8½	2301 19 7	1 3 0
1857	...	...	...	...	...	...	...	...	719 13 10	6 4¾	2724 19 1	1 4 2¼
1858	...	...	...	...	...	...	14 14 0	0 1	787 3 3	6 0½	2625 2 10	1 0 2¼
1859	...	...	...	...	4 15 6	0 0½	843 5 1	6 7¼	769 19 0	6 0¼	2465 7 10	0 19 4
1860	...	...	...	...	21 7 3	0 1¾	167 16 0	1 3	725 6 8	5 5½	3006 11 8	1 2 8¼
1861	...	...	...	...	...	...	137 10 0	1 0¾	700 7 3	5 5¾	2832 9 5	1 2 2½
1862	...	...	...	...	0 4 0	...	111 6 7	1 0¼	870 14 6	8 0¼	2487 17 10	1 2 11
1863	...	...	...	...	...	...	95 2 0	0 8¾	759 13 4	5 11¼	2867 0 10	1 2 5¼
1864	...	...	...	...	4 0 0	0 0¼	90 7 0	0 8¼	764 14 8	5 10½	3656 6 9	1 8 1¼
1865	...	...	...	...	...	...	200 7 0	1 5	747 16 4	5 4	4251 10 2	1 10 4¼
1866	...	...	...	...	4 10 6	0 0¼	161 18 0	0/11½	1106 17 3	6 7½	5173 5 5	1 11 0¼
1867	...	...	...	...	...	...	156 7 0	0 11¼	898 13 3	5 5½	4652 13 10	1 8 3¼
1868	...	...	80 0 0	0 5¾	...	...	97 8 0	0 7	777 1 4	4 8	4086 7 8	1 8 2¼
1869	...	...	383 0 0	2 3¾	0 18 6	...	129 10 0	0 9¼	837 16 10	5 0¾	4449 10 6	1 6 11¾
1870	...	...	334 0 0	1 11¾	15 11 9	0 1	94 10 0	0 6¾	1226 13 10	7 3¾	4275 6 2	0 19 0½
1871	...	...	525 0 0	3 0	8 15 8	0 0½	161 10 0	0 11	826 4 6	4 8½	4483 1 1	1 5 7¼
1872	...	...	370 7 0	2 0	0 12 6	...	505 0 0	2 8¾	1075 12 8	5 9¾	4426 2 10	1 3 11
1873	...	...	584 10 0	3 1¾	2 7 6	...	416 1 0	2 2¾	855 3 9	4 7¼	6626 17 3	1 5 0
1874	...	...	515 10 0	2 8½	19 19 6	0 1¼	486 1 0	2 6½	1031 1 5	5 4¾	8680 15 0	2 5 8¼
1875	...	...	564 0 1	2 8	...	...	899 0 0	4 3¼	1143 16 11	5 5¼	11406 19 1	2 14 8¾
1876	...	...	720 0 0	3 3	36 11 8	0 1¾	187 6 6	0 10	1042 5 11	4 8¼	13555 1 8	3 0 11¾
1877	152 13 0	0 8	564 0 0	2 6	5 2 0	0 0¼	012 1 0	2/8¾	1388 13 8	6 2¼	14012 5 2	3 0 6½
1878	301 15 0	1 3½	840 0 0	3 6¾	30 17 6	0 1½	910 10 6	3 10½	1500 6 2	6 8	14152 0 1	3 4 0
1879	408 2 0	1 7¾	985 13 4	3 11¾	28 11 11	0 1¼	324 10 4	1 3¾	1806 0 0	7 3¾	10727 15 7	2 3 6
1880	622 18 0	2 5¼	932 19 8	3 7¾	44 11 10	0 2	198 11 0	0 9¼	1515 0 8	5 11¼	10378 7 10	2 0 8¼
1881	696 17 0	2 7½	990 12 8	3 8¾	10 1 0	0 0¼	194 13 9	0 8¾	1903 17 8	7 2	10205 7 11	1 18 8¾
1882	690 13 0	2 5¼	845 6 8	2 11¾	4 8 0	...	213 5 8	0 4¾	1418 9 0	5 0	10864 17 6	1 18 4½
1883	880 11 0	3 0	973 15 4	3 3¾	0 5 0	...	228 16 3	0 9¼	1358 0 5	4 7	12414 12 4	2 2 5¼
1884	982 7 0	3 2	1065 4 8	3 5¼	52 1 6	0 2	239 2 6	0 9½	1501 17 10	5 0	14505 0 2	2 6 11¾
1885	983 18 0	3 0¾	1207 0 0	3 9	9 8 2	0/0½	264 5 9	0 9¾	1403 7 8	4 4¼	15918 12 1	2 0 5¼
1886	1089 12 0	3 3½	966 0 0	2 11	77 11 0	0 2¾	75 5 0	0 2½	1786 16 0	5 5	17007 7 0	2 13 5¾
1887	1164 13 0	3 3¾	991 13 4	2 9¾	25 12 5	0 0¾	38 3 0	0 1¼	1007 13 10	4 0¾	20201 15 8	2 17 6
1888	1095 3 0	2 11½	1277 6 8	3 5¼	27 12 9	0 0¾	30 0 0	0 0¾	1636 2 1	4 5	22002 1 5	3 1 3¾
1889	1177 7 0	2 11	1373 13 4	3 5½	3 16 6	...	426 11 0	1 0¾	2010 0 11	5 0¾	25412 0 7	3 3 11¼
1890	1214 14 0	2 8½	1307 0 0	2 11	75 3 5	0 2	883 0 0	1 11¾	2407 6 3	5 4¼	20587 8 5	3 0 5
1891	1375 19 0	2 11¼	1662 6 8	3 6½	3 4 6	...	873 15 0	1 10¼	3182 19 3	6 10¼	20525 4 0	2 10 0½
1892	1678 5 0	3 5	1877 9 4	3 10	18 4 4	0 0½	211 0 0	0 5¼	3030 4 8	7 5	21704 7 10	2 4 3¾
1893	1694 11 6	3 4	1788 6 8	3 6¼	85 13 1	0 2	216 10 0	0 5½	3500 0 1½	7 0½	23793 17 0½	2 0 9¾
1894	1880 3 0	3 9¾	1436 13 4	2 10½	38 19 0	0 1	300 2 0	0 6½	2570 15 11	5 9	24178 18 0	2 8 8¼
1895	1860 10 0	3 8¼	1793 15 7	3 6	32 3 1	0 0¾	384 4 0	0 9	2302 5 5	4 7¼	32434 9 2	3 3 1¼
1896	1875 5 0	3 6¾	1084 13 4	3 2¼	1 11 0	...	371 10 0	0 8½	2571 12 5½	4 10½	44044 10 0¼	4 4 0¾
1897	2027 19 0	3 9¾	1554 6 8	2 10½	9 8 7	...	2150 13 0	4 0	2120 0 0	3 11	54542 7 0½	5 1 2¼

Tables showing the progress of the Society since its re-establishment in 1848. Table No. 1.

EXPENDITURE.	1848 £ s. d.	1849 £ s. d.	1850 £ s. d.	1851 £ s. d.	1852 £ s. d.	1853 £ s. d.	1854 £ s. d.	1855 £ s. d.	1856 £ s. d.	1857 £ s. d.	1858 £ s. d.
Law and Defence of Scale	128 16 6	16 7 5	7 1 6	11 14 1	67 15 4	11 18 0	28 10 0	25 14 11	63 9 3	704 15 8	540 16 5
Unemployed Allowances	186 2 10	187 18 5	200 0 0	176 1 1	232 10 9	94 12 3	51 12 6	730 12 2	238 12 0	200 0 0	346 12 11
Emigration	...	...	...	...	...	250 0 0	350 0 0	100 0 0	100 0 0	...	...
Travelling	36 0 0	51 5 0	43 5 0	50 4 0	31 10 0	29 5 0	40 7 0	38 11 6	76 2 0	65 6 9	63 11 2
Fire	...	...	...	4 18 0	62 8 0	...	...	...	...	...
Committees	34 0 0	32 3 6	32 16 6	35 17 6	35 17 2	38 3 0	43 4 11	81 6 10	69 14 2	93 0 0	101 8 0
Stockholders	...	1 14 7	1 0 6	1 10 0	0 16 6	2 14 0	2 10 0	3 6 4	0 10 0	2 13 3	5 1 3
Rent	30 0 0	20 0 0	20 0 0	20 0 0	20 0 0	20 0 0	20 0 0	30 9 5	26 6 8	27 7 4	38 2 4
Rates and Taxes	...	...	...	...	...	...	...	...	20 4 0	23 13 6	22 10 5
Hire of Halls	8 19 6	7 1 0	7 14 7	6 19 0	6 6 0	6 15 0	9 0 0	12 19 6	17 14 0	20 1 6	8 8 0
Repairs	...	...	...	...	...	...	...	150 8 1	...	17 19 0	67 2 9
Fire Insurance	...	...	...	...	...	...	...	...	...	1 0 0	1 10 0
Printing	20 3 0	18 19 9	23 4 0	15 8 6	15 6 3	9 18 0	24 15 3	68 4 0	64 0 0	77 15 6	92 13 8
Stationery	2 15 11	...	3 9 6	3 11 0	3 3 9	3 2 9	4 10 0	15 8 0	10 1 9	15 5 0	13 12 2
Firing	...	...	...	...	...	...	...	...	20 0 0	18 16 0	24 8 9
Gas	...	...	...	...	...	...	...	4 0 5	21 0 7	34 18 7	27 11 4
Stamps	7 5 5	13 18 11	4 2 4	0 19 11	4 0 0	4 17 8	5 8 8	17 3 5	3 5 4	16 17 11	17 15 4
Medical Charities	...	...	...	...	...	...	...	...	...	...	14 14 0
Trade Circulars	...	...	...	...	...	...	...	...	...	1 9 0	3 7 0
Extraneous Grants	14 8 7	62 6 0	40 0 0	145 0 0	135 0 0	10 0 0	485 0 0	75 13 0	308 15 0	38 6 3	41 13 6
News Department	14 8 7	16 17 9	41 2 1	149 3 10	126 7 10	554 8 11	205 18 9	295 13 8	120 19 9	65 7 8	89 6 6
Library	...	...	...	...	...	...	...	17 10 0	...	...	...
Salaries	118 10 0	109 0 0	109 0 0	109 0 0	104 0 0	114 0 0	111 0 0	107 12 0	166 5 3	249 11 6	219 12 0
Auditors	...	...	0 10 0	1 0 0	1 0 0	1 0 0	1 0 0	...	1 17 0	2 9 0	2 18 0
Miscellaneous	...	13 13 0	6 0 6	...	...	...	...	14 15 9	20 3 8	13 2 10	10 2 0
TOTAL EXPENDITURE	587 1 9	551 5 4	539 7 6	726 8 4	788 12 1	1203 1 7	1383 3 5	1779 7 3	1349 7 2	1689 16 3	1752 17 9
TOTAL INCOME	823 0 9	783 9 10	1028 10 4	1160 10 0	1232 4 4	1595 0 4	1539 4 8	1592 12 9	1446 0 3	1819 4 5	2365 12 4
STATE OF FUNDS	235 19 0	488 16 0	984 14 10	1420 4 7	1862 15 5	2253 11 3	2447 16 3	2270 3 7	2301 19 7	2724 19 1	2625 2 10
NO. OF MEMBERS	1100	1500	1800	1950	2100	2600	2350	2300	2000	2250	2600

Table No. 2.

EXPENDITURE.	1859 £ s. d.	1860 £ s. d.	1861 £ s. d.	1862 £ s. d.	1863 £ s. d.	1864 £ s. d.	1865 £ s. d.	1866 £ s. d.	1867 £ s. d.	1868 £ s. d.	1869 £ s. d.
Law and Defence of Scale	70 16 9	289 1 2	5 8 2	321 16 2	308 8 2	243 14 4	98 16 1	174 19 10	777 0 1	549 4 4	448 10 7
Unemployed Allowances	200 0 0	200 0 0	1034 12 11	677 18 1	393 19 5	1064 14 11	1633 14 0	1800 9 10	2485 9 2	2317 9 0	2686 7 1
Emigration											
Travelling	66 13 0	44 2 0	75 19 6	101 9 6	68 1 0	61 9 9	57 6 6	64 19 0	92 1 6	70 11 6	86 12 6
Funeral		21 7 3		0 4 0		4 0 0		4 10 6		80 0 0	383 0 0
Fire	4 15 6	116 16 6	103 12 2	109 10 0	113 1 0	100 12 10	119 8 0	173 1 9	141 9 0	97 17 0	116 13 0
Committees	150 18 8	5 12 6	58 6 6	3 8 0	6 19 5	3 19 10	6 1 3	6 4 14 6	6 10 8	4 12 5	3 11 5
Stockholders	5 12 0	52 16 6	52 16 6	55 6 6	58 6 0	59 2 0	58 10 0	59 0 0	59 0 0	58 15 0	58 10 0
Rent	53 7 0	20 13 9	20 4 2	24 14 10	17 10 6	20 9 1	19 1 11	23 1 6	23 12 0	23 17 3	23 1 2
Rates and Taxes	18 12 11	13 19 6	11 1 2	7 17 0	9 6 6	23 5 0	25 0 0	99 17 0	17 13 0	5 12 6	13 5 5
Hire of Halls	29 0 6	23 19 9	18 3 11	107 2 7	27 18 11	17 5 0	18 12 2	35 5 0	28 3 0	10 7 0	42 15 5
Repairs		1 10 0	1 10 0	2 0 7	1 1 0	1 10 0	1 1 1	1 1 0	1 1 0	1 1 0	0 12 0
Fire Insurance	27 7 0	60 5 10	44 0 0	90 8 6	63 12 0	57 10 6	61 15 6	191 5 8	69 9 0	71 1 6	77 1 0
Printing	12 16 3	12 3 6	11 17 10	12 19 9	9 14 10	8 2 6	9 10 11	10 2 0	9 10 8	9 6 7	11 11 1
Stationery	21 3 10	21 17 4	15 2 0	21 0 9	20 4 10	21 19 0	15 3 0	17 1 0	22 16 8	18 5 2	21 10 5
Firing	24 19 5	23 12 7	25 6 7	33 3 9	32 17 0	32 9 0	36 8 0	33 9 0	34 2 7	32 15 6	33 13 4
Gas	14 19 5	13 10 0	9 18 3	13 14 0	12 0 8	11 19 2	11 7 8	26 12 0	13 2 7	11 10 6	18 2 0
Stamps	22 1 0	37 16 0	52 10 0	63 0 0	65 2 0	70 7 0	70 7 0	81 18 0	91 1 0	92 8 0	94 10 6
Medical and Trade Charities		4 3 0	1 18 0	0 2 0		3 5 0	3 14 0		3 10 0	3 0 1	4 11 6
Trade Circulars	1 15 0			9 6 7	9 0 6						
Extraneous Grants	821 4 4	130 0 0	85 0 0	48 6 3	30 14 0	20 0 0	130 10 0	80 0 6	65 10 0	5 10 0	35 0 0
News Department	46 17 6	44 12 3	45 6 4	42 0 0	44 14 0	45 12 0	43 17 0	61 18 9	135 13 10	97 11 0	41 2 0
Library	104 11 0	83 8 0	102 12 9	92 9 4	82 8 1	77 19 0	82 17 8	98 18 9	78 10 6	80 14 0	101 13 5
Salaries	223 14 0	215 12 0	217 2 0	229 9 4	242 19 0	253 18 0	219 13 0	239 12 0	245 3 0	229 0 0	250 8 0
Auditors	3 8 0	4 6 0	4 10 0	4 16 0	4 16 0	4 16 0	5 6 0	6 8 0	6 8 0	6 8 0	8 0 0
Miscellaneous	5 13 2	8 6 2	11 12 1	16 7 9	9 8 5	7 15 9	9 6 6	20 10 7	16 16 2	15 1 9	17 10 4
TOTAL EXPENDITURE	1955 9 4	1449 8 2	1955 3 0	2081 17 4	1625 13 11	2214 18 1	2738 0 0	3303 1 5	4473 10 1	3891 19 8	4577 0 6
TOTAL INCOME	1903 7 8	1957 5 4	1779 3 11	1766 4 2	2006 8 2	2957 8 8	3276 15 1	4120 15 0	3859 9 9	3878 14 1	4366 15 2
STATE OF FUNDS	2465 7 10	3006 11 8	2832 9 5	2487 17 10	2867 0 10	3656 6 9	4251 10 2	5173 5 5	4652 13 10	4686 7 8	4440 10 6
NO. OF MEMBERS	2550	2650	2550	2175	2555	2600	2800	3335	3290	3320	3300

Table No. 3.

EXPENDITURE.	1870			1871			1872			1873			1874			1875			1876			1877			1878			1879		
	£	s.	d.	£	s.	d.	£	s.	d.	£	s.	d.	£	s.	d.	£	s.	d.	£	s.	d.	£	s.	d.	£	s.	d.	£	s.	d.
Law and Defence of Scale	1815	10	8	303	14	1	4070	2	8	403	11	8	640	10	9	88	2	3	659	8	11	245	0	9	362	19	5	1700	11	4
Unemployed Allowances	3917	0	9	1822	8	9	1262	10	4	1095	10	5	1258	13	11	848	7	11	2225	17	7	2551	14	0	3263	18	2	5318	2	6
Emigration				113	0	0	232	14	0	191	0	0	203	10	1	122	0	0	103	6	9	55	0	0	73	1	0	271	9	4
Travelling	91	14	6	232	17	0	214	15	0	80	17	6	90	15	0	84	0	0	80	9	0	98	9	0	102	12	0	63	19	6
Superannuation „																						152	13	0	301	15	0	408	4	0
Funeral „	334	0	0	525	0	0	379	7	0	584	10	0	515	10	0	564	0	1	726	0	0	564	0	0	840	0	0	985	13	4
Fire „	15	11	9				0	12	6	2	0	0	19	19	6				36	11	8	5	2	0	30	17	6	28	11	11
Committees	127	15	0	103	6	0	146	6	6	100	13	6	125	0	0	124	19	0	160	15	0	202	12	0	204	15	0	219	19	0
Stockholders	13	19	1	6	6	6	2	18	3	9	9	0	4	13	1	8	15	5	6	1	10	106	18	10	7	1	7	15	12	2
Rent	61	8	0	63	18	4	63	10	8	64	9	0	46	12	1	64	10	0	64	10	0	106	13	0	149	3	6	147	1	3
Rates and Taxes	19	8	4	18	1	11	18	16	8	17	12	6	18	12	1	19	5	10	23	3	11	20	8	6	19	18	6	20	3	11
Hire of Halls	28	7	0	11	3	6	49	6	6	5	12	6	13	8	0	2	9	0	23	2	7	42	5	0	92	5	0	98	5	0
Repairs	228	6	10	4	12	0	40	4	11	2	19	0	54	8	10	139	17	0	9	2	7	59	16	0	66	10	0	35	10	0
Fire Insurance				0	12	0	0	12	0							0	16	0	0	16	0				11	6	0	0	16	0
Printing	142	14	0	124	3	0	121	8	0	96	14	6	161	4	6	133	0	0	95	3	6	193	16	0	307	19	6	414	5	3
Stationery	13	11	3	11	8	6	13	11	6	10	4	6	8	10	8	10	2	6	5	17	7	13	2	0	43	8	6	19	11	9
Firing	20	0	0	16	5	6	23	6	8	26	0	6	23	3	8	22	0	6	23	16	2	22	16	6	18	18	6	21	0	4
Gas	19	3	8	25	5	6	32	4	8	35	14	7	41	14	0	40	6	3	39	1	6	41	2	0	42	7	1	46	2	4
Stamps	26	7	8	21	10	0	26	12	1	12	5	2	20	5	10	16	19	4	12	15	5	23	10	10	27	12	1	30	2	7
Medical and Trade Charities	94	10	0	94	10	0	105	0	0	106	1	0	106	2	1	135	9	0	143	17	0	204	15	0	181	13	0	187	19	6
Trade Circulars	3	10	6	3	3	0	7	13	0	10	16	8	3	3	0	10	17	0	10	10	0	10	12	0	10	12	0	10	12	6
Extraneous Grants				67	0	0	400	0	0	280	0	0	380	0	0	705	0	0	10	10	0	374	0	0	700	0	0	80	0	0
Trade Union Congress													3	3	0	59	0	0	32	19	6	33	6	0	29	6	6	56	11	4
Eagle Street Land																						1016	13	4	22	6	0	172	7	0
News Department	54	10	6	41	4	6	53	5	10	73	10	0	91	16	4	54	13	6	52	14	0	54	13	0	51	6	0	59	12	3
Library	149	5	1	96	17	2	98	15	8	108	13	0	110	6	5	170	9	7	180	18	0	174	8	11	119	10	10	190	3	3
Salaries	296	12	0	257	6	0	285	0	0	257	16	0	264	4	0	295	4	0	307	2	0	356	14	0	376	15	0	436	14	0
Auditors	6	8	0	6	8	0	6	8	0	6	8	0	6	8	0	6	8	0	6	8	0	7	0	0	7	1	8	9	0	8
Miscellaneous	16	19	7	19	5	11	72	1	2	49	1	0	23	13	8	21	12	0	23	5	0	47	18	3	29	1	8	35	0	2
TOTAL EXPENDITURE	7497	3	6	3998	5	1	7718	12	6	3594	4	10	4251	1	8	3755	1	8	5066	16	5	6689	6	9	7494	11	4	11084	1	4
TOTAL INCOME	6462	1	9	5112	5	0	7536	14	3	5709	9	3	6421	4	5	6138	15	9	6950	19	0	7110	10	3	7264	6	3	7711	6	10
STATE OF FUNDS	3375	6	2	4483	1	1	4426	2	10	6626	17	3	8680	15	0	11496	19	1	13555	1	8	14012	5	2	14182	0	1	10727	15	7
No. OF MEMBERS	3350			3500			3700			3700			3800			4200			4445			4795			4800			4930		

Table No. 4.

EXPENDITURE.	1880 £ s. d.	1881 £ s. d.	1882 £ s. d.	1883 £ s. d.	1884 £ s. d.	1885 £ s. d.	1886 £ s. d.	1887 £ s. d.	1888 £ s. d.
Law and Defence of Scale	229 12 10	534 9 6	713 15 8	661 0 2	575 16 1	1202 11 2	1325 0 2	743 4 0	459 1 2
Unemployed Allowances	4997 17 0	4985 3 0	4800 15 4	4140 3 11	4005 6 10	5267 17 11	5442 4 2	4743 10 10	5544 6 5
Emigration	166 1 8	231 0 0	208 0 0	219 0 0	201 0 0	191 0 0	266 0 0	177 0 0	150 0 0
Travelling	66 11 6	59 8 0	37 5 0	69 0 0	54 10 0	114 10 0	53 0 0	75 10 0	66 15 0
Superannuation	622 18 0	696 17 0	690 13 0	880 11 0	982 7 0	983 18 0	1089 12 0	1164 13 0	1095 3 0
Funeral	932 19 8	990 12 8	845 8 0	973 15 4	1065 4 0	1207 0 0	996 0 0	991 13 4	1277 6 8
Fire	44 11 10	10 1 0	4 8 0	0 0 0	52 1 0	9 8 2	77 11 0	25 12 5	27 12 9
Committees	183 7 0	232 14 0	153 0 0	142 13 0	158 4 0	100 5 0	99 10 0	141 10 0	126 4 0
Stockholders	6 17 0	25 13 6				13 15 0			3 16 0
Rent	138 12 11	128 7 0	127 5 10	130 0 0	130 0 0	130 0 0	130 0 0	130 0 0	130 0 0
Rates and Taxes	21 2 2	26 2 10	24 13 6	23 0 0	24 1 0	28 6 4	34 13 3	35 1 7	36 16 11
Hire of Halls	67 12 6	111 0 6	43 12 0	54 10 0	48 17 0	43 8 0	37 19 0	43 8 8	49 1 0
Repairs	151 10 6	94 7 0	97 12 11	80 13 7	122 7 6	43 1 0	85 16 2	104 7 8	95 7 2
Fire Insurance	6 1 0	6 1 0	11 6 0	6 1 0	6 1 0	6 1 0	5 5 8	6 1 0	6 1 0
Printing	254 15 6	451 19 6	225 11 8	260 17 11	270 5 9	261 1 7	540 16 8	320 8 6	355 4 0
Stationery	16 18 11	20 3 7	17 15 8	8 10 6	12 6 8	10 10 5	11 10 8	13 3 0	8 15 5
Firing	17 0 6	22 11 10	15 17 7	10 7 1	12 2 5	13 7 0	9 11 0	11 13 6	16 4 0
Gas	47 18 6	37 7 4	35 17 7	31 12 5	27 0 5	26 3 10	26 14 0	21 6 3	18 10 11
Stamps	29 12 2	31 17 5	27 7 7	22 13 10	37 18 11	32 12 0	40 16 0	27 16 5	37 19 3
Medical Charities	123 18 0	131 10 0	131 5 0	136 10 0	147 0 0	157 10 0	168 0 0	173 5 0	210 0 0
Trade	15 15 0	15 15 0	15 15 0	15 15 0	15 15 0	15 15 0	15 15 0		15 15 0
Trade Circulars	10 12 0	12 19 0	6 0 6	12 4 0	12 4 0	12 4 0	12 4 0	12 4 0	12 4 0
Extraneous Grants	30 0 0	15 0 0	30 0 0	30 0 0	35 10 0	32 2 0	75 5 5	38 3 0	30 6 0
Trade Union Congress	38 18 0	32 13 9	36 5 8	46 11 3	40 17 6	41 5 0	53 15 5	26 14 8	66 6 0
London Trades' Council						17 13 0	16 15 0	17 10 8	15 11 11
Eagle Street Land	2 17 6	13 2 6	5 5 2	3 4 0	82 15 1	8 8 0	174 13 0		
News Department	60 17 6	67 4 6	70 4 9	57 16 0	88 13 0	70 8 8	65 14 0	62 8 6	106 15 4
Library	50 6 5	114 17 6	103 12 9	85 12 3	116 3 2	121 17 1	150 10 10	132 7 1	101 0 3
Salaries	389 8 4	475 15 0	439 0 0	439 0 0	439 0 0	460 15 0	491 0 0	516 5 0	541 2 0
Auditors	9 10 0	9 0 0	9 0 0	9 0 0	9 0 0	9 0 0	9 0 0	9 0 0	9 0 0
Miscellaneous	25 9 5	45 1 0	29 12 1	29 7 2	52 0 7	25 7 2	40 6 4	18 6 7	25 9 10
TOTAL EXPENDITURE	8819 13 5	9628 10 4	8955 14 6	8579 15 1	8824 11 6	10657 1 8	11520 18 1	9781 10 1	10591 15 0
TOTAL INCOME	8948 5 8	9765 10 5	9955 4 1	10129 9 11	10915 5 4	15067 2 7	13207 16 0	12383 18 3	13082 2 9
STATE OF FUNDS	10378 7 10	10265 7 11	10864 17 6	12414 12 4	14505 6 2	15918 12 1	17007 7 0	20201 15 8	22692 3 5
No. OF MEMBERS	5100	5300	5660	5850	6175	6435	6585	7025	7400

K 2

Table No. 5.

Expenditure.	1889 £ s. d.	1890 £ s. d.	1891 £ s. d.	1892 £ s. d.	1893 £ s. d.	1894 £ s. d.	1895 £ s. d.	1896 £ s. d.	1897 £ s. d.
Law and Defence of Scale	624 12 0	522 8 2	1718 4 11	1104 0 4	1666 4 0	1106 19 3½	890 15 10	991 3 8	409 14 3
Unemployed Allowances	5188 11 0	5539 0 0	10638 13 8	11906 6 4	11865 11 6	1683 13 1	1193 18 6	10518 11 5	10080 16 5
Emigration	285 0 0	138 0 0	178 0 0	319 0 0	209 0 0	213 0 0	168 11 8	128 0 0	175 0 0
Travelling	86 0 0	88 0 0	321 15 0	307 0 0	395 15 0	516 15 0	361 3 0	313 0 0	183 0 0
Superannuation	1177 7 0	1214 14 0	1375 19 6	1678 5 9	1694 11 6	1886 8 0	1892 10 0	1875 5 4	2027 19 6
Funeral	1373 13 4	1307 0 0	1662 6 8	1877 4 4	1788 6 8	1436 13 4	1793 15 7	1684 13 4	1554 0 8
Fire	18 16 6	75 3 3	18 4 0	18 4 4	85 13 1	38 10 6	32 3 0	18 10 0	9 8 7
Committees	229 3 0	301 12 0	640 18 0	597 4 4	545 0 0	400 8 6	317 16 0	433 0 0	288 19 6
Ballot Scrutineers	...	...	3 4 8	5 10 0	...	...	59 1 0	48 0 0	60 6 6
Stockholders	2 12 0	...	...	...	5 0 0	1 10 0	5 10 0	5 5 0	3 7 0
Rent	130 0 0	130 0 0	130 0 0	126 15 0	65 0 0	...	...	...	...
Rates and Taxes	38 17 11	37 12 11	39 18 3	144 12 0	193 5 8	156 0 0	182 3 4	215 12 6	159 9 2
Hire of Halls	53 5 0	56 14 6	94 2 6	103 13 0	135 6 4	87 0 0	75 0 8	130 16 0	105 15 6
Repairs	72 13 0	96 5 6	67 1 0	8 13 0	69 1 10	190 6 11	123 18 4	101 18 2	63 3 2
Fire Insurance	6 1 0	6 1 0	6 1 6	22 14 6	32 9 8	27 0 0	27 0 0	27 0 0	27 0 0
Printing	489 17 7	631 0 3	989 5 1	1079 3 6	678 15 9	928 13 3	553 10 9	1147 17 4	495 6 11
Stationery	27 11 3	37 10 7	32 8 1	39 1 4	29 16 9	28 6 0	27 0 9	40 5 0	29 6 1
Firing	11 2 6	11 12 6	28 11 0	31 12 0	22 10 0	22 10 0	10 0 0	20 0 0	15 5 2
Gas	18 0 0	17 1 0	25 8 8	32 18 10	60 14 8	61 13 0	...	...	...
Electric Light	...	...	...	...	...	29 17 0	106 14 1	0 7 11	0 1 8
Stamps	60 15 11	80 19 1	88 18 5	88 4 9	82 18 4½	88 15 3½	83 7 7½	85 9 0	69 10 8
Medical Charities	220 10 0	261 0 0	241 10 0	241 10 0	244 13 0	244 13 0	255 3 0	94 7 10	81 19 4
Trade	15 15 0	31 10 0	31 10 0	31 10 7	31 10 0	31 10 0	31 10 0	267 15 0	279 6 0
Trade Circulars	12 4 0	13 10 4	12 13 4	12 13 7	12 13 4	12 13 0	2 4 11	3 3 0	31 10 0
Trade Emblems	...	...	...	...	...	376 2 0	...	...	4 6 4
Extraneous Grants	426 11 0	633 15 0	873 15 6	261 0 0	271 10 0	199 5 4	150 0 6	257 5 0	2159 13 0
Trade Union Congress	68 0 3	49 15 0	91 13 6	56 0 0	41 0 0	42 0 0	34 10 2	41 0 0	41 10 11
London Trades' Council	14 13 0	103 12 6	137 12 0	147 17 0	110 11 0	147 4 0	112 12 0	109 4 0	120 1 0
Eagle Street Land	...	...	...	...	...	...	...	...	...
News Department	173 6 6	161 10 1	154 6 3	240 13 6	236 8 1	268 4 0	163 6 3	209 8 4	238 12 7
Library	29 8 0	93 10 2	90 8 8	32 5 4	51 15 2½	63 12 2	81 1 1½	59 13 4	...
Newspapers, &c.	...	...	...	...	...	...	...	...	54 14 4
Salaries	630 0 0	690 5 0	762 12 0	768 19 2	718 12 7½	774 19 4½	723 9 5	709 19 5½	678 4 6
Auditors	9 0 0	9 0 0	51 10 6	101 5 6	110 6 0	106 14 6	100 1 0	91 7 0	89 15 6
Caretakers	...	...	...	...	...	78 0 0	78 0 0	84 0 0	81 0 0
Miscellaneous	32 17 4	38 15 11	114 0 9	151 0 2	80 6 6½	98 11 7½	101 4 3	68 6 10	100 17 5
Total Expenditure	11502 4 5	12377 10 1	20612 18 0	21594 16 7	23824 0 3	26349 13 10	20464 0 0	19809 0 6½	19803 2 11
Total Income	14242 1 7	16532 17 11	18253 14 2	19554 11 2	29935 2 5½	26956 9 6	28519 10 8	32609 10 3	29843 17 10
State of Funds	25432 0 7	29587 8 5	26525 4 9	21704 7 10	23763 17 0½	24378 18 6	32434 9 2	44044 10 6½	54542 7 0¾
No. of Members	7955	8910	9350	9798	10151	10011	10280	10558	10780

Grants in Aid of Kindred Organisations.

Year	Organisation	£	s.	d.
1849	Defence Committee, Sheffield	20	0	0
,,	Bookfolders and Sewers, London	30	0	0
1850	Typographical Society, Edinburgh	20	0	0
,,	Typefounders	20	0	0
1851	Typographical Society, Cork	50	0	0
,,	Do. do. Manchester	20	0	0
,,	Do. do. Paris	15	0	0
1852	Tin Plate Workers, London	100	0	0
,,	Engineers	100	0	0
,,	Stamp Abolition Committee	10	0	0
1853	Typographical Society, Birmingham	10	0	0
1854	Do. do. Belfast	50	0	0
,,	Factory Operatives, Preston	320	0	0
,,	Cork Cutters' Society	75	0	0
,,	House Painters, Dublin	10	0	0
,,	Friendly Societies' Act Committee	5	0	0
,,	Testimonial to Mr. Boyett	25	0	0
1859	Flint Glass Makers, London	25	0	0
,,	Building Trades' Operatives	560	0	0
,,	Typographical Society, Sheffield	100	0	0
1860	Do. do. Clonmel	16	0	0
,,	Do. do. Waterford	10	0	0
,,	Building Trades' Operatives	60	0	0
,,	Typefounders, London	20	0	0
,,	Boot and Shoe Makers, London	20	0	0
1861	Umbrella and Parasol Silk Weavers	20	0	0
1862	Operative Stone Masons' Society	30	0	0
1863	Typographical Society, Turin	30	0	0
1864	Spade Makers, Stourbridge	10	0	0
,,	West End Boot Closers' Association	10	0	0
1865	United Flint Glass Cutters	30	0	0
,,	Typefounders, London	30	0	0
,,	Typographical Society, Plymouth	30	0	0
,,	Operative Lace Makers, Notts	20	0	0
,,	Operative Brick Makers, London	10	0	0
,,	Testimonial to Mr. Speak	10	0	0
1866	File Grinders, Sheffield	30	0	0
,,	Amalgamated Malleable Ironworkers	30	0	0
,,	Pattern Makers' Society	20	0	0
1867	Tailors' Protective Assoc., London	10	0	0
,,	Miners of Derbyshire and Notts	30	0	0
1869	Cotton Operatives, Preston	30	0	0
,,	Amalgamated Trades' Committee	5	0	0
1871	Thick Iron and Steel Wire Drawers	20	0	0
,,	Engineers, Newcastle	30	0	0
,,	Cigar Makers' Society, Antwerp	15	0	0
1872	Scottish Typographical Association	250	0	0
,,	Typographical Society, Edinburgh	150	0	0
1873	Lace Makers, Nottingham	30	0	0
,,	Provincial Typographical Assoc.	20	0	0
,,	Scottish do. do.	230	0	0
,,	London Trades' Council	20	0	0
,,	T.U.C. Parliamentary Committee	10	0	0
1874	Agricultural Labourers, Leamington	130	0	0
,,	Amalgamated Labour League, Boston	130	0	0
,,	Provincial Typographical Assoc.	40	0	0
,,	Typographical Association, Naples	20	0	0
,,	Operative Ropemakers, London	30	0	0
,,	Ship Boat Builders' Society	10	0	0
,,	Defence Fund (Master and Servant Act)	20	0	0
1875	Elastic Braid Hands, Leicester	30	0	0
,,	Plimsoll Defence Fund	100	0	0
,,	Alliance Cabinet Makers, London	30	0	0
,,	London Trades' Council	5	0	0
,,	T.U.C. Parliamentary Committee	30	0	0
,,	Miners and Ironworkers, Monmouth	530	0	0
,,	Provincial Typographical Assoc.	10	0	0
1876	T.U.C. Parliamentary Committee	10	10	0
,,	Testimonial to Mr. Geo. Howell	10	10	0
,,	Testimonial to Mr. Geo. Odger	10	0	0
1877	Typographical Association, Brussels	130	0	0
,,	Do. do. Limerick	20	0	0
,,	Nail Forgers' Association, Bromsgrove	20	0	0
,,	Silk and Wool Printers, Dartford	20	0	0
,,	China Clay Labourers, St. Austell	10	0	0
,,	Hand-Mule Spinners, Bolton	30	0	0
,,	Operative Stone Masons, London	100	0	0
,,	Nut and Bolt Makers, Darlaston	30	0	0
1877	Miners' Association, West Lancashire	10	0	0
1878	Miners' Association, Longton	10	0	0
,,	Do. do. Northumberland	60	0	0
,,	Typographical Society, Dublin	500	0	0
,,	Do. do. Paris	130	0	0
,,	T.U.C. Parliamentary Committee	10	0	0
1879	Kent and Sussex Labourers	30	0	0
,,	Engineers' Relief Fund, London	30	0	0
,,	Warpers' Society, Bury	6	0	0
,,	Gold Beaters' Society, London	5	0	0
,,	T.U.C. Parliamentary Committee	15	0	0
1880	Journeyman Hatters, London	20	0	0
,,	Typographical Association, Naples	10	0	0
,,	T.U.C. Parliamentary Committee	15	0	0
1881	Do. do. do.	20	0	0
,,	Nail Makers' Assoc., Birmingham	5	0	0
,,	Potters' Federation, Burslem	10	0	0
1882	Typographical Society, Waterford	5	0	0
,,	Tobacco Pipe Makers, Glasgow	10	0	0
,,	Cotton Spinners, Lille	10	0	0
,,	Sheet Iron Workers, Stourbridge	5	0	0
,,	T.U.C. Parliamentary Committee	15	0	0
1883	Do. do. do.	15	0	0
,,	Typographical Association, Vienna	10	0	0
,,	File Cutters' Association, Sheffield	10	0	0
,,	Porcelain Workers, Limoges	5	0	0
,,	Philanthropic Coopers, London	5	0	0
1884	Weavers, N.-E. Lancashire	10	0	0
,,	Testimonial to Mr. H. Broadhurst, M.P.	10	10	0
,,	Boot and Shoe Riveters, London	10	0	0
,,	Elastic Braid Hands, Leicester	5	0	0
,,	T.U.C. Parliamentary Committee	15	0	0
1885	Do. do. do.	15	0	0
,,	Cocoa Fibre Mat Makers, Suffolk	10	0	0
,,	Miners, S. Yorks and N. Derbyshire	10	0	0
,,	Testimonial to Mr. Lloyd Jones	2	0	0
,,	Industrial Representative League	10	0	0
1886	T.U.C. Parliamentary Committee	15	0	0
,,	Typographical Society, Turin	10	0	0
,,	Typographical Federation, Paris	40	0	0
,,	Tin Plate Workers, London	10	0	0
,,	Vellum & Parchment Makers, London	5	0	0
,,	Testimonial to Mr. J. Burnett	5	5	0
,,	Nottingham Branch T.A.	5	0	0
1887	Chain Makers, Cradley Heath	10	0	0
,,	Testimonial to Mr. W. Dronfield	3	3	0
,,	Iron Trades, Bolton	10	0	0
,,	Leeds Trades' Council	5	0	0
,,	Typographical Society, Essen	10	0	0
,,	T.U.C. Parliamentary Committee	19	0	0
1888	Do. do. do.	15	0	0
,,	Bryant & May's Matchmakers, London	51	4	0
,,	Typographical Society, Cork	10	0	0
1889	Mr. A. G. Cook's S. B. Election Expenses	31	6	0
,,	Dock Labourers, London	300	0	0
,,	Small Wire Drawers, Halifax	10	0	0
,,	Lace Workers, Nottingham	10	0	0
,,	Tailors, East London	10	0	0
,,	Indiarubber Workers, Silvertown	10	0	0
,,	British Typographia, London	10	0	0
,,	Typo. Society, Perth (W. Australia)	10	0	0
,,	Do. Christiana	5	0	0
,,	Do. Vienna	5	0	0
,,	Tramway Employés, London	5	0	0
,,	Tea Operatives, London	5	0	0
,,	Portmanteau Makers, London	5	0	0
,,	Bass Dressers, London	5	0	0
,,	Cigarette Makers, London	5	0	0
,,	Sailors and Firemen, Liverpool	5	0	0
,,	T.U.C. Parliamentary Committee	20	0	0
1890	Do. do. do.	20	0	0
,,	Australian Workers	250	0	0
,,	Gas Workers, London	200	0	0
,,	Barge Builders, London	40	0	0
,,	Boot and Shoe Riveters, London	10	0	0
,,	John Burns' Wages Fund, London	10	0	0

Grants in Aid of Kindred Organisations—Continued.

Year	Organisation	£	s.	d.
1890	Lace Makers, Calais	10	0	0
,,	Printers' Labourers, London	10	0	0
,,	Typographical Association, Zurich	10	0	0
,,	Stick Dressers, London	10	0	0
,,	Elastic Web Weavers, Leicester	5	0	0
,,	Electrical Engineers, London	5	0	0
,,	Allen's Chocolate Girls, London	5	0	0
,,	Barrett's Chocolate Girls, London	5	0	0
,,	Councillor Athey's Fund, Stratford	5	5	0
,,	Testimonial to Mr. H. Slatter, J.P.	5	5	0
,,	Sausage Skin Dressers, London	5	0	0
,,	Scale Makers, London	5	0	0
1891	Typographical Association, Berlin	510	0	0
,,	Do. do. Vienna	110	0	0
,,	Carpenters and Joiners, London	110	0	0
,,	Railway Servants, Scotland	40	0	0
,,	T.U.C. Parliamentary Committee	20	0	0
,,	Brick Makers, Cowley	10	0	0
,,	Coopers, London	10	0	0
,,	John Burns' Election Fund, London	10	0	0
,,	Omnibus Workers, London	10	0	0
,,	Weavers, Bradford	10	0	0
,,	Bass Dressers, London	5	0	0
,,	Cab Drivers, London	5	0	0
,,	Hosiers, Leicester	5	0	0
,,	Packing Case Makers, London	5	0	0
,,	Potters, London	5	0	0
,,	Tailors, London	5	0	0
1892	Bookbinders, London	100	0	0
,,	French Polishers, London	5	0	0
,,	Wire Weavers, London	5	0	0
,,	John Burns' Wages Fund, London	10	0	0
,,	Tyne and Wear Engineers	10	0	0
,,	Durham Mining Federation	10	0	0
,,	Printers' Labourers' Union, London	10	0	0
,,	Brush Makers' Union	10	0	0
,,	Leather Dressers' Union	5	0	0
,,	Bookfolders' Union, London	5	0	0
1893	Workmen's Exhibition, London	10	0	0
,,	Dockers' Union, Hull	10	0	0
,,	Glassworkers' Union	5	0	0
,,	Chain Makers' Union, Cradley Heath	5	0	0
,,	Wilson Defence Fund	5	0	0
,,	T.U.C. Parliamentary Committee	20	0	0
,,	Miners' Federation	200	0	0
1894	Womens' Trade Union Association	5	0	0
,,	T.U.C. Parliamentary Committee	20	0	0
,,	Horse-hair and Fibre Workers, London	5	0	0
,,	Cab Drivers' Union, London	5	0	0
,,	Match Girls' Union, London	5	0	0
,,	John Burns' Wages Fund, London	10	0	0
,,	Scottish Miners	5	0	0
1895	Glassblowers' Union	5	0	0
,,	National Boot and Shoe Union	10	0	0
,,	T.U.C. Parliamentary Committee	11	0	0
,,	John Burns' Wages Fund, London	10	0	0
,,	Austin Election Fund	10	0	0
,,	Electrical Union, London	5	0	0
,,	Carmaux Glass Workers, France	10	0	0
,,	International Congress, London	5	0	0
1896	T.U.C. Parliamentary Committee	11	0	0
,,	Plate Glass Bevellers' Union, London	5	0	0
,,	Builders' Labourers' Union, London	10	0	0
,,	Steadman Wage Fund, London	5	0	0
,,	Russian Strike Fund	10	0	0
,,	Builders' Labourers, Leeds	2	2	0
,,	Fancy Leather Workers (on account)	50	0	0
,,	Testimonial to Mr. G. Shipton	10	0	0
,,	Carpenters' Union, Brussels	10	0	0
,,	Do. do. do.	20	0	0
,,	Cab Drivers' Union, London	10	0	0
,,	Quarrymen's Union, North Wales	10	0	0
,,	Dock Labourers, Hamburg	10	0	0
1897	T.U.C. Parliamentary Committee	11	0	0
,,	Spindle Makers, Oldham	10	0	0
,,	John Burns' Wages Fund, London	10	0	0
,,	Barry Trades' Council	10	0	0
,,	Farriers' Union, London	10	0	0
,,	Typographical Society, Cape Town	10	0	0
,,	Testimonial to Mr. Geo. Howell	10	0	0
,,	Machine Minders, Edinburgh	10	0	0
,,	Federation Committee, T.U.C.	10	0	0
,,	Penrhyn Quarrymen	340	0	0
,,	Engineers (Amal. Soc.)—Grants	780	0	0
,,	Do. do. —Levies	868	0	0
		£10,379	0	0

DATES OF PRINCIPAL EVENTS.

1770 Daily newspapers contained sixteen small columns, from 18 to 20 ems long primer in width. The "Daily Advertiser" contained twelve columns, 25 ems long primer in width. Wages: full hands, 27s.; supernumeraries, 13s.; galley, 2s. 2d. (5d. per thousand) and over-hours 6d. Most of the papers were small folios, and mainly produced in book houses.

1776 Reports of Parliamentary Debates first appeared in daily papers.

1777 Seven morning papers were being published, and eight three times, one twice, and two once per week.

1778 First Sunday paper produced, followed in a few weeks by a second, a third appearing during the following year. Weekly paper hands received 24s.

1780 New daily paper started, differing in appearance from those in existence.

1784 New journal started, into which minion type was introduced for the first time.

1785 Circular issued (April 6th) requesting an advance of ½d. per thousand (book-work then paid for at 4d. per thousand).

1786 Book hands' advance granted from January 1st; 'stab hands' wages varied from £1 1s. to £1 7s.

1786	In March, daily paper hands received an increase of 4s. 6d. Wages: full-frame hands, £1 11s. 6d.; supernumeraries, 15s., galley, 2s. 6d.
——	Eight daily papers, eight three times a week, two weekly, and three Sunday journals were being published.
1788	First daily evening paper started; composition paid for at morning paper prices.
1791	Second evening paper started, on same terms.
1793	Book hands claimed (January 14th) payment for head and direction lines, also en and em quadrats at sides. Former charge allowed, March 11th.
——	Introduction into daily papers of French rules and small capitals, the long *s* being discarded.
——	Circular issued by newsmen (April 4th) claiming advance of 4s. 6d. per week for morning and evening paper hands, owing to changes in method of production. Signed by 145 newsmen, the request being supported by 281 book hands.
——	Employers' proposals accepted that morning paper hands should receive a rise of 4s. 6d. and evening paper hands 2s. 6d. per week, making the wages of former 36s., supernumeraries 17s., galley 2s. 10d.; the latter 34s., supernumeraries 16s., galley 2s. 8d.
——	Newsmen (with support of bookhands) resisted attempt to introduce apprentices and turnovers into daily paper offices.
1801	Book hands received advance of one-sixth, from January 1st.
——	Morning paper hands received advance of 4s. (£2), supernumeraries 2s. (19s.), galley 3s. 2d., assistants 9½d. per hour; evening paper hands 3s. (£1 17s.), supernumeraries 1s. (17s.), galley 2s. 10d., assistants 8½d. per hour.

1801   First Trade Society of Compositors formed, "to correct irregularities, and to bring the modes of charge from custom and precedent into one point of view, in order to their being better understood by all concerned."

1809   Morning paper hands' wages raised to £2 2s. (galley 3s. 4d.), evening paper hands to 38s. (galley 3s. 2d.)

1810   Book hands received advance of one-seventh from May 1st. Agreed upon at a General Meeting of Master Printers, held at Stationers' Hall, April 16th.

——   Newsmen's claim for further advance of 6s. (morning) and 5s. (evening) refused by employers.

——   Book hands resolved that no member should apply for employment upon a newspaper during the dispute.

——   On May 14th (after notices had almost expired) the employers granted the increases: Morning paper hands £2 8s., supernumeraries 23s., galley 3s. 10d. (9d. per thousand), assistants 11½d. per hour. Evening paper hands £2 3s. 6d., supernumeraries £1 1s. 6d., galley 3s. 7d. (8½d. per thousand), assistants 10½d. per hour.

——   Eleven members were prosecuted by the proprietor of a daily newspaper on an indictment charging them with conspiracy in connection with the dispute, and were imprisoned for twelve months—one member dying in Newgate.

1811   Dispute *re* introduction of an apprentice into an evening paper office, lasting six weeks.

1813   Morning papers of 20 columns became almost general.

1816   Introduction of nonpareil type into newspapers.

——   Dispute through employers claiming that it should be composed at the same price as minion. One penny per thousand extra eventually granted.

1816	"Three Herrings" Society formed, September. Meeting place: Bell Yard, Temple Bar. Mr. W. Smith, Secretary.
1820	London Daily Newspaper Society established.
1826	London General Trade Society of Compositors established, May 1st, for trade purposes exclusively. Meeting place: "Twelve Bells," Bride Lane, Fleet Street. Mr. R. Gilbertson, Secretary.
1832	Union Committee appointed by Trade Societies, to consider questions affecting periodical publications.
——	Delegate Meeting held at "Red Lion," Red Lion Court, Fleet Street, October 9th. Present—138 from book and 2 from news offices.
1833	Union Committee advocated amalgamation of existing societies.
1834	London Union of Compositors formed, with 1,543 members.
——	Delegate Meetings held quarterly (one in twelve being appointed from each office), at which a Trade Council of 24 was elected, to deal with disputes, holding office for three months.
——	Trade Council met every Tuesday evening, and on the last Saturday in each month (to deal with news questions), at the "Red Lion," from 8.0 to 10.30. Expenses of refreshment not to exceed sixpence each. Mr. R. Thompson, Registrar; Mr. W. Bayne, Secretary.
——	Dispute with an employer re Charge of Appeal Cases. July.
——	Dispute re Charge of Wrappers.
1835	First Annual Meeting held in Theatre of London Mechanics' Institution, February 2nd. Membership, 1,700; total receipts, £450 19s. 9½d.; dispute payments, £245 8s. 1d.; funds in hand, £66 9s. 7d.

1835	Deputation attended meeting of Northern Union, Manchester, June 27th.
——	Presentation of Petition to Parliament to obtain Repeal of the Stamp Duties.
——	Establishment of Relief Fund for Tramps.
1836	Re-establishment of Master Printers' Association, December 8th. Mr. G. Woodfall, Chairman ; Mr. W. M'Dowall, Secretary.
1838	Mr. E. Edwards appointed Secretary of London Union of Compositors, in succession to Mr. Bayne.
——	Business of Society transferred from " Red Lion " to No. 9½, Bouverie Street, Fleet Street (" London Compositors' Office.")
——	Mr. R. Thompson appointed as Registrar and Office-Keeper.
——	Petition presented to Parliament against Mr. Serjeant Talfourd's Copyright Bill.
1842	Business of Society transferred to " Falcon " Tavern, Gough Square, Fleet Street.
1845	National Typographical Association established, February 1st. Divided into five districts—the South-Eastern comprising London. Corresponding Secretary, Mr. J. Backhouse ; South-Eastern District Secretary, Mr. R. Thompson.
1847	Arbitration Committee (eight representatives of employers and employed) met at Freemasons' Tavern, Great Queen Street, on July 9th, the sittings being continued until November 4th.
1848	RE-ESTABLISHMENT OF LONDON SOCIETY OF COMPOSITORS, January. Mr. E. Edwards, Secretary. Meeting place: " Falcon " Tavern, Gough Square.
——	Voluntary Provident Fund established, March. Subscription : 2d. per week. Benefit : 8s. per week for fifteen weeks.

1848	News Department established, June. Mr. C. Tugwell, Secretary.
1850	Fire Benefit re-established, January.
——	Mr. Edwards resigned the Secretaryship, March; succeeded by Mr. J. Boyett, May 1st.
1852	Compositors' Emigration Aid Society formed, September 25th. Subscription: 3*d*. per week.
1853	Amalgamation of Old Daily News Society with London Society of Compositors, March.
——	National Typographical Emigration Society formed, and ceased to exist same year.
1854	Mr. Boyett resigns Secretaryship; succeeded by Mr. W. Cox.
1855	Society's business transferred to No. 3, Racquet Court, Fleet Street, June.
——	Arbitration Committee (three employers and three journeymen, with a barrister as chairman) appointed. Rules came into operation on January 1st, 1856.
1856	Meeting of Arbitration Committee at Freemasons' Tavern, August 5th.
——	Amalgamated Committee (Book and News) reported upon system of working in newspaper offices.
1857	Death of Mr. W. Cox, January 2nd. Mr. J. C. Crabb appointed Secretary *pro tem*.
——	Mr. W. Beckett appointed Secretary; Mr. J. Shand as Assistant-Secretary.
——	Compositors' Permanent Sick Fund established.
1858	Judgment of Exchequer Court given in Society's favour (Standing Advertisements in Wrappers, etc.), February 25th.
——	First Grant made to Medical Charities.

Dates of Principal Events.

1859   Recorder of London (Mr. Russell Gurney) decides against Society in an action *re* charge of table matter (Voting Lists, etc.).

1860   Petition Fund Account established.

1862   Tramping System of Relief (1*d*. per mile) rejected.

1863   Providend Fund incorporated with Trade Society.

——   Mr. Beckett resigns the Secretaryship through ill-health.

——   Maximum Subscription increased to 6*d*. per week.

1864   Mr. H. Self appointed as Secretary, April 6th.

1866   Advance of Wages Memorial presented to employers. Agreement signed in November. Rise of ½*d*. per thousand, 'stab wages increased to 36*s*., and working hours reduced to 60 per week.

——   Providend Benefit increased to 10*s*. per week.

1868   Death Allowance added to Society's benefits.

——   Maximum Subscription increased to 7*d*. per week.

——   Mr. J. Borer appointed as Assistant-Secretary and Librarian, in succession to Mr. J. Shand (deceased).

1869   Sick members' subscription reduced to 1*d*. per week.

1870   Dispute and loss of three offices through resisting reduction of Scale prices.

1871   Half-pay Provident Benefit introduced.

——   Emigration and Removal Allowances added to benefits.

——   Names of Unemployed Benefit Recipients first printed with Quarterly Report.

——   Printers' Art Union Association formed, September.

——   Nine Hours' Movement entered upon.

1872   Memorial presented to employers, January.

——   Working hours reduced to 54 per week, and advance of ½*d*. per thousand secured, March.

1872	Mr. C. Baker appointed as News Secretary, in succession to Mr. J. Roberts (deceased).
1874	Memorial presented to Daily and Weekly Newspaper Proprietors.
——	Weekly paper hands secured overtime charge of 3*d.* per hour after 60 hours' work.
1876	Delegate Meetings first held in Memorial Hall, Farringdon Street.
1877	Superannuation Benefit established.
——	'Stab "Line" Bill Question referred to Arbitrator (Mr. Thomas Hughes, Q.C.), whose award was given on July 3rd.
——	Freehold Land in Eagle Street (for building Society House) purchased for £3,616 13*s.* 4*d.*
1878	Mr. C. J. Drummond appointed as Assistant-Secretary; Mr. T. J. Thompson as Chairman.
——	Provident Allowance increased to 12*s.* per week, and to extend over 16 weeks (previously 13).
1879	Rules of the Society first Registered.
1880	Mr. R. Lee appointed as Chairman, in succession to Mr. Thompson (resigned).
——	Special Committee appointed to inquire into Financial Condition of Society.
——	Subscription permanently increased to 8*d.* per week.
——	Superannuation Benefit (maximum) reduced to 6*s.* per week.
1881	Mr. A. G. Cook appointed as Librarian and Housekeeper.
——	Appointment of four Trustees (Messrs. J. Melhuish, J. R. Meyer, C. J. Radley, and R. J. Townsend) in place of Stockholders.
——	Resignation of Mr. H. Self (through ill-health), to whom a retiring allowance of £50 per year was granted.
——	Mr. C. J. Drummond appointed as Secretary; Mr. C. Morley as Assistant-Secretary.

Dates of Principal Events. 159

1882 Mr. G. W. Banks appointed as Assistant-Secretary.
1883 Mr. J. Woozley elected as Treasurer, in place of Mr. J. C. Yeoman (deceased).
—— Special Committee appointed to devise a scheme for the Re-constitution of the Executive.
1884 Society took part in Trade Procession in connection with the Great Reform Demonstration.
1885 Society affiliated with the London Trades' Council.
—— Society House and Reading Room closed from Monday to Friday at 9.0 (previously 10.0), and on Saturdays at 3.0 (instead of 4.0) o'clock.
1886 Secretary appointed upon Royal Commission on the Depression of Trade and Industry.
—— Mr. R. W. Minter appointed as Chairman, in succession to Mr. R. Lee (deceased).
—— Printers' National Art Union wound up.
—— Eagle Street Land sold.
1887 Finance Committee appointed.
1888 Ballot upon Eight-hours' Question (resolution of Swansea Congress).
—— Half-pay Provident Allowance abolished.
1889 Second Ballot upon Eight-hours Question.
—— Trade Committee first elected by Ballot.
—— Mr. C. W. Bowerman appointed as News Secretary, in succession to Mr. C. Baker (resigned).
—— Conference upon "Slating" Question in Daily Newspaper Offices.
—— Superannuation Allowances (maximum) increased to 8s. per week.
—— Mr. H. G. Weir elected as sub Assistant-Secretary, but did not enter upon the duties of the office.

1890	Messrs. T. E. Peacock and W. Thorne elected as Assistants.
——	News Committee elected by Ballot.
——	Advance of Wages Movement entered upon.
——	Sub-Committee appointed to Revise the Scale.
——	Memorial presented to Employers, November 24th.
——	Mr. Henry Self died (December 30th), aged 74.
——	Allowance of £50 per year continued to Widow.
——	Chartered Accountants appointed to Annually Audit Society's Accounts.
1891	Conference re Advance of Wages convened at Stationers' Hall, January 26th, its sittings terminating on February 12th.
——	Revised Scale signed on February 18th, to come into operation on March 1st.
——	Mr. W. Crespin appointed as a Trustee in place of Mr. Townsend (resigned).
——	Minute to Scale (Matters of Interpretation) signed on September 1st.
——	Special Committee appointed to deal with the "Call" Book.
——	Committee appointed to inquire into Working of Daily Paper Offices.
——	Purchase of Freehold Premises (Nos. 7–9, St. Bride Street) for £10,500, August.
1892	Dispute with Daily Paper Office re Terms of Working Composing Machines, January.
——	Special Committee appointed to Reconstruct the Executive, and to revise and re-arrange the Rules.
——	Resignation of Messrs. R. W. Minter (Chairman) and C. J. Drummond (Secretary).
——	Mr. R. F. McBean elected as Chairman, and Mr. C. W. Bowerman as Secretary, March 25th.

Dates of Principal Events.

1892	Mr. C. J. Drummond appointed a Trustee in place of Mr. C. J. Radley (deceased).
——	Mr. J. Connal elected as Assistant-Secretary, April 11th.
——	Mr. T. Sanders appointed as News Secretary.
——	Subscription permanently increased to 9*d*. per week, May 13th.
——	Inquiry into Systematic Overtime, July.
——	Grant made towards establishing a Trade Journal.
——	"Printing News" published, August.
——	Committee instructed to inquire into "Gift" Question.
——	Terms agreed upon for Working Type-Distributing and Composing Machines.
1893	Trade Dinner at Cannon Street Hotel (to commemorate acquisition of new Society House), January 28th.
——	Opening of St. Bride Street Premises, January 30th.
——	Non-Provident Relief Fund raised (in consequence of rejection of Provident extension), April.
——	Mr. J. Galbraith elected as Chairman, in succession to Mr. McBean (resigned).
——	Committee reported upon "Gift" Question.
1894	Subscription permanently increased to 10*d*. per week, January 6th.
——	Trade Emblem adopted.
——	Subscription increased to 1*s*. per week for a period of twelve months.
——	First Conference upon Composing Machine Question, Anderton's Hotel, June 7th.
——	Discussion in House of Commons upon Mr. T. Lough's motion *re* Stationery Office Contracts, August 18th.
——	Committee appointed to Inquire into Working of the various Sub-Committees.

1894	Non-Provident Relief Funds raised, May and November.
1895	Mr. R. Dent appointed a Trustee, in place of Mr. J. Melhuish (superannuated).
——	Subscription permanently increased to 1s. per week, April.
——	Special Committee appointed to devise the best means of decreasing the number of Unemployed Members, May.
——	Delegates to Trades Union Congress first elected by ballot.
——	Select Committee of House of Commons appointed to Inquire into the Stationery Office Contracts, June.
——	Second Conference upon Composing Machine Question, Anderton's Hotel, December.
1896	Select Committee reported to House of Commons, June.
——	Third Conference upon Composing Machine Question, Salisbury Hotel, July.
——	Reception to Representatives of Continental Typographical Societies attending International Congress, July.
1897	Meeting of Arbitration Board (Interpretation of Machine Rules), Salisbury Hotel, January.
——	Complimentary Trade Dinner to Messrs. T. Lough and M. Austin, February 20th.
——	Scheme of Federation with Kindred Societies adopted, November.
——	Superannuation Allowances Increased (in commemoration of the Society's Jubilee), coming into operation on January 1st, 1898.